PRACTICAL
MUSICAL
CRITICISM

By

OSCAR THOMPSON

Music Critic, *New York Evening Post*
Six Seasons, 1928–34
Associate Editor, *Musical America*
First Instructor in Music Criticism at the Curtis Institute

WITMARK EDUCATIONAL PUBLICATIONS
DEPARTMENT OF M. WITMARK & SONS
NEW YORK

PRINTED IN THE UNITED STATES OF AMERICA
BY THE STRATFORD PRESS, INC., NEW YORK

To Mr. W. J. Henderson, the greatest music critic America has produced —though *he* would accord that honor to *another*—this workaday volume on the critic's profession is deferentially and affectionately dedicated.

March 31, 1933.

FOREWORD

The author is well aware of the elementary nature of what is set forth in this outline of music criticism. He knows that if his audience were to be composed of his colleagues of the Metropolitan press he would be guilty of the most gratuitous citing of what is obvious, trite and quotidian. But extensive experience in newspaper-writing away from New York, as well as in Manhattan, has convinced him that over the country there is a real need for some such discussion of critical first principles and their workaday application.

Further experience as instructor in music criticism at the Curtis Institute in Philadelphia has fortified this conviction, because of what was revealed by his students as to current misconceptions of the function, the aims, the obligations and the ordinary procedure of criticism. Finally, the almost daily incidents in which the Metropolitan critic is called upon for some word of advice to an aspirant hopeful of adopting criticism as a vocation, and in doubt as to what he can do to prepare himself for this work, or how he can obtain employment if he is in some measure already prepared, would appear to justify putting into print what has to be repeated verbally over and over, to those seeking this advice.

It should be clear at the outset that this is not a book on musical appreciation. It assumes a workable knowledge of music in all of its forms on the part of the reader. Furthermore, let it be confessed unblushingly that this is not a book of "the higher criticism," whatever for music that may be. It is not a book on aesthetics. It is not a book of musical analysis. It has to deal primarily with a form of journalism, not as practiced in Italy or Germany, England or France, but in the United States. Its modicum of theory is only a generalization of current practice. Its aim is to make an open book of the profession for those who have only hazy notions as to what the work of a music critic involves. The author feels no need to apologize for the absence from these pages of anything that could be termed a philosophy of criticism. His concern has been with the *modus operandi*. The many repetitions of certain basic considerations are intentional, on the theory that misconceptions are seldom swept away with a single whisk of the broom. To repeat, the book is elementary. So, as the author sees it, is the need.

TABLE OF CONTENTS

BOOK ONE

THE PROFESSION

WHY CRITICISM?

If there were no newspapers, no magazines, no books, no printing presses, it is obvious that we still would have music criticism.

On occasion, a musician, goaded by some injustice, real or fancied, clinches his teeth about the assertion that criticism should not be. He means the kind that finds its way into type.

An hour later, or five minutes before, his friend, his pupil, his sister's growing daughter, his Saturday bootblack, hears him saying just what he thinks about a pianist, a symphony concert or some cancrizanic Schönberg.

How would it look in print? Would it be fairer, would it be more moderate, more considered, more juridical, more lenitive with the milk of human kindness than that which caused his gorge to rise?

Aside from good, bad and indifferent, "constructive" and "destructive" (words about words!), there are two really distinguishable kinds of criticism: That which is printed and that which is said.

How do they compare as to casualness on the one hand and deliberation on the other? Which is the more likely to be offhand and hasty; which to compel some measure of caution, reflection and corroboration?

Who must stand behind the spoken phrase, whether in praise or denigration? Where is it anchored? How is it to be referred back to, when the flare-up it produces entails the usual dispute as to just what was said and how it was intended? Without a record, the jewel of consistency might as well be paste—or putty.

The printed word does many things for a critic. It puts him on his guard against himself. Reversing a decision is no way to retain prestige, self-respect or readers. Responsibility's way of making conservatives of radicals in politics is well known. The critic who does not write more conservatively than he talks is the exception. Talk is cheap, libel suits may not be. To be sure, most criticism is "privileged". But irresponsibility in the columns of any periodical, daily, weekly or quarterly, has a way of getting a careless thinker or reckless writer into difficulties.

It is the common lot of the music editors of newspapers to receive letters about criticism—from critics of critics—that no stretching of ethics, personal, public, critical or journalistic, can justify in print. If the reviewers had written as rashly in the criticism under fire, a likely result would have been some vacant thrones.

But is the harm of this sort of impulsive judgment confined to what appears in print? Since when has word of mouth ceased to be a power for good or ill, in a world that spends most of its waking hours either talking or listening? That much of mass impression with respect to music, and many specific impressions on the part of individuals, are formed by the passing of verbal opinions is obvious. Reputations are made and shattered, misconceptions and untruths are perpetuated, biases and personal antagonisms are engrafted on the green stock of formative notions, second-hand and third-hand and hundredth-hand criticisms are circulated endlessly. No one is responsible. No way can be found of returning to the starting point so as to get at the first opinion. Rumors, wraiths, will-o'-the-wisps of praise or condemnation, cartoons, grotesqueries, gargoyles of thought; these are substituted for what once may have been a sly but friendly "dig" or just the usual final platitude on the breaking up of a box-party.

Criticism is opinion and opinion is criticism. To contemplate such a void as would exist if society could be bereft of its opinions, is to feel, indeed, what star-gazers have described as "the cosmic chill". Surely not the mountains of the moon could be more desolate in their barren waste.

Serious people think and say unserious things. Considering the manner in which unwritten criticism circles the world, filters into preoccupied ears, bores into reluctant intellects, colors, distorts and exaggerates in its infinite variety of contacts, can any musician, martyred or no, seriously believe that professional music criticism should be done away with, now and forever?

Faulty, variable, erratic, sometimes ill-formed, sometimes harsh or unjust, always something in which the human equation asserts a prepotent influence, professional criticism yet has its anchor in the written word. What that word is today it will be tomorrow and ten years hence. To repudiate it is perilous. Courageous the critic who will publicly confess a change of mind. That can happen and happen handsomely. But the knowledge, that if it happens too often there may be a longing for another critic in the chair, is sufficient to cause most critics to seek to fortify their views in every way they can. There is a responsibility not to be evaded jauntily when comparisons are made from day to day between the written opinion of one critic and the written opinion of another, and between the written opinion of both and the unwritten opinion of the few (or the multitude) of those cultured or curious individuals who feel called upon to discover what the critics had to say.

Responsibility goads conscience and conscience goads the faculties that make for efficiency, whether they have to do with the collation of materials, the acquisition of knowledge, straight and hard thinking, or deft and illuminative writing. To stand by what is said means to be as sure of one's ground as can be in the face of circumstances not always the most favorable, but certainly no more unfavorable for the critic who writes for the public than the critic who talks for—well, whom do we talk for, as we come out of a concert hall? Ourselves or those who are with us?

Criticism is! There's the short and the long of it. To abolish it would be to put a Maxim silencer on all report, a gag in every mouth, a shroud on every opinion bursting to be born into the world. To attempt to balance the good against the harm it does, is beyond the scope of these remarks. Whether most of the so-called "harm" is not good in disguise is one of the red rags of critical controversy. But surely, this much is beyond cavil: trained criticism is more likely to work for good than untrained criticism; disciplined judgment promises more of what is sound and fair than undisciplined judgment; the professional is more to be trusted than the amateur.

THE FIELD

Music criticism, as will be emphasized repeatedly in this book, is a form of literature concerned with music; not a form of music that has flowed over into literature. It is a thing of words, sentences, paragraphs and the thoughts they are intended to convey, not of notes, bar lines, timbres and sonorities. Unless he be his own publisher, the critic must sell his wares. Music that is never played is not so forlorn as criticism that is never read.

Let us survey, then, the field. The critic may write for newspapers, he may become a member of the staff of a musical journal, or he may contribute to any and all such publications as consider the subjects he chooses to discuss as of special or general interest. He may go in for program notes, for books of essays, for tomes on musical appreciation, for biography, even for musical novels. But all of these latter are corollaries or extensions of his true critical function. The daily newspaper, and to a lesser extent, the musical journal, will, for the purposes of this discussion, constitute the field.

In New York, Boston, Philadelphia, Chicago and those other American cities which are nearest these in importance as hubs of musical life, the field is a shrinking one. Consolidations of newspapers have eliminated many first desks. There were only about half as many first critics in New York in 1933 as there were in 1919. The critical aspirant whose goal is the Manhattan newspaper whirl needs a supreme faith in himself as a chosen tool of Providence, if he is not to be beaten down by discouragement early in his quest. Exclusive of the so-called tabloids, which may or may not give more attention to music as they change with a changing day, there are three morning newspapers and four evening which employ critics and assistants-to-critics to review daily the music of New York. This does not include the Brooklyn or other borough papers, the Jewish, German and other foreign language dailies. The morning papers referred to are the Times, Herald Tribune and American; the evening, the Sun, the Post, the World-Telegram and the Journal.

Seven possibilities then, at the most, for the man or woman who fixes an eye on the desks occupied at this writing by Messrs. Downes, Gilman, Liebling, Henderson, Thompson, Sanborn and Weil.* Would there be much incentive to enter the medical profession, or the legal, or politics, or the ministry, or to prepare for a career as an educator, if, in a city of seven millions, there were room for but seven men at the top? Nor is the possibility of doing second-string criticism, in the capacity of assistant to the head of the department, one on which

---

* Since the above was written Henriette Weber has become critic of the *New York Evening Journal,* in succession to Irving Weil, who died Aug. 26, 1933.

high hopes can be nourished. Add another fourteen or fifteen names, at the most, to those of the first desk writers, and the entire story, so far as these seven newspapers is concerned, has been told. Nor are the emoluments of these places such as would justify long waiting and persistent seeking. The assistant must expect to hear much inferior music; together with performances which would never be endured willingly by his chief. There is little joy in listening to some fourth-rate fiddler or singer at the very hour some cherished symphony, opera or treasure of chamber music is being performed elsewhere—for others but not for you—out of sight and out of hearing—but not out of mind!

Fortitude is required to go night after night to the musical leavings and be permitted only now and then a share in the purple patches of the year. To have to try to write interestingly about what was anything but interesting in performance, with an allotment of space that seems to preclude anything but a mere news report, the while the first critic expounds and expands for a column or more on a subject that gives play to his erudition and his command of language, is something of martyrdom for the youth who would hitch his wagon to a star. Every reviewer of background and experience knows that it is much easier to treat important events *in extenso* than it is to deal succinctly and readably with the season's everlasting small fry. The literary flair will take care of the one; a highly developed technique is required for the other.

There are not many cities in America where music

criticism is taken so seriously that newspapers can assure
full-time employment for writers concerned with music
alone. In the few where criticism is on much the same
plane as in New York there have been newspaper consolidations to limit further the possibilities. The apex of
the pyramid tapers more sharply than at any time in at
least a half century of American journalism. If critics
died or resigned every year the opportunities would be
formidably few, as compared to those in most lines of
human endeavor. But critics are rather notoriously long-
lived, as illustrated by the impressive records of Henry
E. Krehbiel, Henry T. Finck, William J. Henderson,
Philip Hale and Charles Pike Sawyer; to name but five,
three * of whom are at their desks today (1933), and
each to be credited with more than forty years of distinguished service. In the freshness of his style, Mr.
Henderson may be regarded as the youngest writer on
music in New York. No wonder something like a blank
wall seems to confront the critical aspirant, perhaps
admirably equipped, who is eating his heart out for opportunity to prove his worth.

Some compensation for the shrinking Metropolitan
field is to be found over the country. As America becomes more and more conscious that it is growing up,
newspapers become aware of the sorry manner in which
they have relegated music to the list of necessary evils.
Some effort is being made to have reviews written intelligently, if not with any particular authority. The "sob-

---

* Diminished to two by the retirement at the beginning of the 1933-34
season of Philip Hale, as critic of *The Boston Herald*.

sister" and the society editor no longer suffice. Either some member of the staff is assigned to write of music, in connection with other duties, because he is believed to have an acceptable knowledge of his subject, or reviews are farmed out to musicians who have some secondary ability as writers.

Bitter experience has taught many a managing editor to avoid the latter expedient, except as a last resort. The most biased, harsh and impolitic reviews ordinarily are those penned by the small-town or city musician, committed to some particular "method" or "school", an ultra-conservative or one determined at all costs to be "modern", and likely to be so absorbed in successions of chords or the blending of so-called "registers" as to be utterly unable to see the forest for the trees. Almost inevitably there is trouble over the purely journalistic requirements. The copy is written long-hand or typewritten badly on impossible paper. There is unending worry as to whether reviews will be in the office at the time specified. Once they have arrived, they have to be scanned closely for possible libel. Edited with much gnashing of teeth, they come out dull as ditchwater. And the next day, the town's musicians who have happened to disagree accuse the reviewer of playing favorites, declining to take from one of their own number what they would feel compelled to take from some mere reporter on the newspaper, however scant his musical training.

The picture drawn is purposely the extreme one, but the author has had his days of wandering journalism in many cities and he knows whereof he speaks. He has

seen a steady change for the better in the cultural growth
of these cities. More writers with sufficient musical background to enable them to write sense about music are
finding employment in newspaper offices. Save for the
accumulated experience which is second in importance
to no other factor in giving authority to the writing of
the Metropolitan critic, there may well be reviewers
among these who are basically as able as the men writing
in New York. They cannot transcend their field. They
must adapt themselves to that field and they cannot
write as severely or (if the term be allowed) as bril-
liantly as their Metropolitan confreres. Civic promotion,
such as is necessary for the upbuilding of a local orchestra or the maintaining of an artist course, sometimes in-
terferes with blunt utterance. Policies that have to do
with civic growth and civic pride sometimes lay their
hand on music departments, as on all other newspaper
departments in cities that are full of the booster spirit,
in a manner that would be intolerable in New York. The
critic must adjust himself to this situation or he becomes a loose spoke in the wheel. But the more knowledge and ability he has, both as a critic and a journalist,
the better he can make even his "policy" reviews play a
real part in the musical growth of the community. The
rhapsodic blurb does no one any good. The reasoned,
soundly buttressed and moderately expressed review,
even though it treads warily as to insufficiencies, and
seeks out rather obviously the better aspects of everything undertaken, *can avoid falsification,* at the same
time that it is informative and preparatory for better

things. There is a growing field then, for the newspaperman who has a special knowledge and is content
to adapt that knowledge to the needs of newspapers and
cities not yet of the first magnitude. He must expect to
do other work and, in most instances, to find that it is
music—not the copy desk, the city hall beat, the clubs
and supper places, the make-up grind, or whatever it is
he is called upon to combine with music—that is of secondary concern, to be fitted in as best it may with the
necessary duties; duties that may sometimes result in
conflicting demands upon his time. Olin Downes * has
said that a few competent critics scattered throughout
the country would do more good than any other new
factor in our musical life. We have schools and teachers
in plenty, artists in abundance, and more orchestral and
other ensemble ventures than we have found the means
safely to finance. But we still need intelligent writing
about music in cities that have a musical life of their
own and are deriving no good from the puffs and effusive
"write-ups" that their newspapers print because this is
the best they can command.

---

* Olin Downes, since 1924, music critic of *The New York Times*.

HOW CRITICS ARE CHOSEN

Every Metropolitan critic is besieged by young men and women eager to become critics. Over and over they ask one question he finds difficult to answer. How does one become a critic? He can only reply that there is no rule, custom or tradition about it. Critics are chosen in many different ways and for perhaps as many reasons. But who selects the critics, who employs them? Again the answers are various. Some one high on the staff of a newspaper assumes this responsibility. In many instances it may be the managing editor; in some, the city editor. In others, the editor-in-chief. Occasionally even the publisher—or, since this is the world it is, the publisher's music-loving wife! Perhaps no two instances will be found that exactly duplicate one another as to the manner in which the choice was made. There are "influences", back-stage and back-stairs, in all professions; and journalism is no exception. But if "pull" has opened a door now and then, "pull" never made a competent critic. The sort of favoritism that foists a nonentity on the readers of a newspaper usually paves the way for a resounding fall. There are too many competent writers clamoring for every post to make it probable that an incompetent can hold on long.

A new Metropolitan critic comes on the scene when there is a vacancy. Few and far between as these vacancies are, they do occur, by reason of death, retirement, resignation or transfer to some other work. Removal for cause has been so rare as to minimize hope in that direction for the aspirant waiting to step into an incumbent's shoes. A flood of fresh applications is to be expected the moment the news of any vacancy gets abroad. These may or may not be consulted. Many other applications have been on file for weeks, months, even years. Quite possibly, someone already has the "inside track"—perhaps an assistant to the critic on this, or another paper; perhaps a critic in another city; perhaps a friend of the managing editor who has been kept in mind over a considerable period for just such an opening; perhaps someone whose contributions to the magazines or the musical journals have met with a friendly eye. Perhaps for the sake of "a big name", a guest critic is called in from across the Atlantic. Perhaps a copy desk man, a reporter or an editorial writer who has been plugging away at some other work is given a chance for which he has been importuning his chief until he has become the office nuisance. The appointment may be a purely experimental one for the sake of a breezy style, a writing personality. Or, less likely, a conductor, a composer, or a musical educator out of a job, may have prevailed upon the highest-ups to employ him to bend a bulging brow to those profundities of music they fancy lie beyond the capacity of any mere journalist properly to grasp. Some one gets the job. The reasons may be ob-

vious or they may be devious. The appointment may be
justified at once or remain inexplicable until the last
trump shall sound.

If this is all very discouraging to the gifted and stu-
dious youth, devoted to the highest ideals and convinced
that merit must win, let him pause to consider the similar
incertitudes of the other walks of life he regards as his
alternatives. In the long run, it is not this lack of any
set procedure in the selection of critics, but the scarcity
of positions to be filled over a period as long as ten or
twenty years that must be regarded as the great hurdle
in the path of the prospective critic.

If anything like regularity of selection could be established, it is probable that more assistants would be pro-
moted to the first desks. The goal of the aspirant would
then be to obtain employment as an assistant, whatever
the sacrifices this might mean as to salary and the types
of musical events likely to occupy most of his listening
hours. Even with irregularity the rule, there still is every
reason for the youth who would be a critic to obtain an
assistant's position if he can. There, again, the odds are
heavily against him. These positions, too, are discourag-
ingly few. And if this first step should be successful, the
odds still are against eventual promotion to the critic's
desk. The infrequent, however, is not the impossible.
The saying, "Once an assistant, always an assistant"
has been proved untrue in various instances. Two of the
most noted critics America has produced were for some
years assistants to men whose subsequent fame was no
greater than theirs. It would not be difficult to find other

instances in which first desks were filled by promotion. On the face of things, these instances should be more frequent than they are. In all that pertains to journalism and routine, the assistant is ready for the larger task; whether he has the ability for it may not be judged fairly until he actually has taken on its responsibilities. His state of preparedness is strongly in his favor.

Any other applicant will be able to make out a better case for himself, if, like the assistant, he can establish that he is a practical journalist. He should know how to prepare copy so that it will be accepted without question as newspaper copy. He should have acquired the knack of writing to meet space requirements and within the limitations that will confront him as to time. He should know how to tell a story as well as voice an opinion. If he is at home in a newspaper city room, if he can read and correct proof and make editorial corrections after the proof room has done its best or worst, if he is prepared to write headlines and subheadings that will "fit" as to the count of units and pass muster for what they say, if he has some measure of comprehension as to what is involved in newspaper make-up and what compositors, galley boys, stereotypers, pressmen and even circulation promoters and advertising solicitors are for, so much the better for him.

The friction that is eliminated, the steps that are saved, the increased respect that is shown to music as a department of the newspaper when the critic is a part of it rather than a species of contributor to it, are almost unanswerable arguments in behalf of journalistic training. Exceptions are not to be denied. There have been distinguished critics who have violated every article of the journalist's code, save that, we trust, of professional honesty. To emulate these, however, is scarcely the way to convince a harried managing editor that an applicant should have the job; or, having it, that there is any vital necessity for this man's services being retained.

Persistence has landed more than one aspirant in a critical chair after repeated rebuffs had given him ample reason to seek his livelihood in some other capacity. Cleverness in presenting one's case counts in newspaper offices, as elsewhere. Letters of recommendation from influential quarters supported by proofs of the applicant's capabilities in the form of published articles, may mean much or little; they have about the same chance of receiving serious consideration as have similar recommendations and proofs in commercial life, politics or the army. Unless the published articles reveal unfitness for the work, they rarely will be prejudicial. They may have attention. They may be helpful. It is logical to make use of them. But there may be no disposition on the part of the employer to wade through documents.

The odds are heavily against a selection that is not based on a previous acquaintance with the man or his capabilities more extensive than would be indicated ordinarily by the need of such letters and samples of handiwork. But the odds are heavy all along the way. In the face of all the discouragements that can be brought to bear, the fact remains that new critics *do* come up—there *is* a place at rare intervals *for some one.*

QUALIFICATIONS FOR CRITICISM

The completely qualified critic does not, cannot exist. He would be the sum total of human knowledge, the sum total of human experience. If he knew all there is to know about music, that would be but a beginning. If he knew everything about literature, about painting, about sculpture, about the dance and about the theatre, he would be a superman among his fellows, but there would be much more for him to learn. But he is out of the question. In his place is to be considered an individual who, at best, is only fractionally equipped for his profession; but who, in most instances of ordinary day-to-day competence, has something to contribute to the knowledge and experience of readers less informed than he, or with less training and aptitude for the formation of judgments. The critic must, first, be read. Once read, he must be found to have said something in some degree interesting, informative or stimulating to the thought of the reader. It is of little good for him to put into print what any other listener might have said. True enough, readers often admire most the reviews that seem to say precisely what they believe they would have said. To be agreed with, increases one's self-respect. But if the review is, in fact, a good one, it has gone beyond merely agreeing with the opinions of the listener; it has crystallized and concentrated them, it has served as a precipitant and a resolvent. Shadows have been converted into clear images. The reasoned has replaced the intuitive.

Ability and adaptability are to be assumed as prerequisites for success in any profession; they may be native or acquired, but their absence must, in the long run, defeat the critic whose musical knowledge might otherwise fit him for his task. Emotional instability and a tendency to strong and fixed mental biases, for and against, make difficult the path of the analyst and the adjudicator. Runaway enthusiasms and easily aroused antagonisms are hindrances that may beset a reviewer throughout his career. A controlling cynicism is likely to be an even greater handicap than the Pollyanna outlook that mistakes cabbages for roses. The critic needs a mind of exceptional fluidity and one of the penetrating kind that plumbs to essentials, recognizes them for what they are and separates them at once from unessentials. The critic needs physical vitality and steady nerves. Taste he can acquire, together with musical knowledge and the technique of writing; but for certain types of minds and emotional natures the dispassionate, evaluative, analytical approach, if not altogether impossible, is immeasurably more difficult than for others. It is for those who can reason about music, even when their feelings have been strongly stirred, that the critical profession holds some promise of success, whatever the exceptions that can be adduced wherein exceptionally brilliant

writers or pungent personalities have outshone their
more sober fellows by reviews as scintillant as they were
prejudiced and unsound.

Granted the ability that is doubtless discoverable in
a multitude of individuals out of all proportion to a
handful of situations, the qualifications that are acquired rather than native begin with the knowledge of
notes and words and stretch away into infinity. Nothing
in preparation for criticism is ever fully achieved. Nothing is ever an approximation of what ought to be
achieved. Everything that is acquired opens new doors.
Whatever the progress along one or a hundred paths,
there is endlessly more beyond, with each minor by-way
leading into a plexus of other radiations. The more the
reviewer knows, the more there is he knows he can never
know. This ought to keep him humble in the practice of
his profession. Arrogance based on knowledge as frac-
tional as that of the most learned reviewer in the world
is rightfully objectionable to all his fellows. The dignity
and poise of scholarship are not irreconcilable with true
humility. There need be nothing abject or apologetic
about frank acknowledgment that the ball within the
grasp compares but minutely with the cosmos that lies
beyond.

Of acquired qualifications, that which may be said to
come first in importance is the one that, ordinarily, the
individual possesses last. This is the experience of hearing much music—and by "much" must be understood a
quantity that can place him on something like an equal
footing with his critical confreres and give him a distinct

advantage over a majority of his readers. Granting that quick perceptions and a fresh viewpoint may count for more than lethargic repetition and dull familiarity, there is likely to be something rather preposterous about a youth who is hearing his first Wagner cycle holding forth on the subject for the edification of Metropolitan Opera subscribers who may have been listening to the Ring music-dramas for ten, fifteen and twenty years. With the situation reversed, the reviewer who has just heard the Beethoven Seventh Symphony performed four times in one week by as many different conductors leading as many orchestras, weary though he may be of that particular symphony, is apt to have something to pass on to the reader who attended only one of these performances. The actual practice of the profession, in this respect, qualifies the critic as no other studies or preparation can do. It is automatically self-educating. The early rapture may never be recaptured, but it is the dint of endless hearings, often unwelcome ones, that most develops for the critic his capacities for judgment and his technique for passing that judgment on, a technique of analytical thought before it becomes a technique of words.

But there must be a beginning, and unless recruits for the critical profession are to be enlisted solely from among the middle-aged, with a preference given either to those who have been active as musicians, or to the not altogether desirable type of dilettante who had nothing to do but store up musical experience while his fellows were grinding out a livelihood which permitted them no such luxurious pursuits, other qualities must be accepted in lieu of the advantages of years of listening. The gramophone, used in conjunction with score-reading, will help the beginner to get over much ground; though he needs to be warned against permitting a first "reading", with which he may become even too familiar, to become his measuring rod for tempi, sonorities, and various details of performance. The radio, too, has its uses for those who know how to flee its debasements. Book and classroom studies have to be converted into auditory sensations in some way. No short-cut can take the place of the toilsome road of the daily practice of the profession, but the more of actual listening, how-so-ever achieved, the young writer can bring to bear upon his earliest reviewing, the more entitled he is to an opinion and the expression of that opinion.

Score-reading, the ability to play on the piano an orchestral score, the faculty of being able to examine a score and from the printed page draw some conclusions as to its nature and its craftsmanship when there is nothing to give it sound, are advantages no aspirant should from choice forego. But they can never take the place of actual performance. Judgments should be formed by the ear and not the eye. Paper dexterity that does not "sound" is common enough. As music, it simply does not count. Many a barren page, as it stands printed on the staves, has been known to blossom as the rose when its timbres were brought to life. Ever and always, music that is worthy of the name was written to be heard; not to be seen.

Taste, like knowledge, like judgment, can be cultivated and prospers with experience. Fairness, open-
mindedness, courtesy too, respond to careful nurture.
In at least a rudimentary stage, these are prior requi-
sites in the equipment of any one entering the profession. A liberal education, good breeding, the ordinary
attributes of the gentleman, even in a day that scarcely
prides itself upon these, and the orientation with respect
to life that we describe as the "cultural", play their part
inevitably in fitting the critic for his task. His knowledge
of the technique of music and of musical literature
should be extensive, though there is no reason to expect
him to be a composer or an adequate performer on any
instrument. The ability to play the piano and to sing
(at least as well as most conductors sing!) is to be regarded only in the light of a convenience in the examina-
tion of scores. Trite as it is, and numerous as are the
versions which have altered it in the telling, there is no
aphorism that sums up the situation better than this one:
It is not necessary to be able to duplicate the crowning
achievement of a hen to be a good judge of an egg. Professional tea-testers doubtless know far more about the
varieties of tea than the Chinese coolie who makes it
grow.

To be a good judge of the musical egg, to have a deli-
cately discriminating taste in this matter of musical
teas (heaven forbid), the critic needs all the book knowledge he can absorb, whether from the scores themselves,
from tracts and treatises, from the critical writings of
others, from historical and biographical studies and the

vaster reaches of literature in which music does not figure at all. The longer he practices his profession, the more the critic realizes that he would need several lives to encompass the reading he could easily prescribe as necessary to his background if all the presses should be halted forever and not another book brought into the world.

Young or old, callow or mellow with long experience, sound or erratic, kindly or acidulous, impartial or given to exploiting hobbies, superficial or profound, the critic must be read. Otherwise he serves no purpose except that of meaning something to himself. The ability to write is second to no other qualification. If he has a style too awkward, too laborious, too stilted, or too commonplace to quicken interest in what he has to say, he should be diverted to some other activity. Among the fundamentals that will have to be stated and re-stated, even to the point of tiresome reiteration, in this outline of practical criticism, this one cannot be too strongly emphasized. Criticism is literature. It is not music. Music criticism is literature dealing with music. It is not music somehow transliterated into words. The critic expresses himself in words, sentences and paragraphs, not in notes, rests, key signatures and musical forms. In contradiction to the musician, he writes for the eye, not for the ear. He may be a journalist, he may be an essayist, he may be a maker of books. But it is all literature, good, bad, high, low, fascinating or dull; still literature and not music. Vital among the critic's qualifications is the literary gift. It is a flair not to be acquired by playing the 'cello, by tapping the timpani, by training choir boys or working wonders with a little ash or maple stick or even an ivory-and-ebony gift-baton. The timpanist, we are told, must love his drums. The critic, equally unashamed, must possess and cultivate a love of words.

THE FUNCTION OF CRITICISM

Criticism, as practiced in the world of today, particularly with respect to the daily newspapers, has one clear function, so central and dominating that all others may be regarded as subsidiary or supplementary. That function is to *hold up a mirror* to what has been composed or performed and to the performance. The mirror is an intensifying one. It reflects the essentials, eliminates the unessentials. Its purpose is to present a clear picture of what the music is, with its good points and bad, or what the performance was, with its salient characteristics, meritorious or otherwise. It aims to be informative, to cut through confusions and distractions to the heart of things, to clarify and crystallize impressions for those who were listeners, to convey an intelligible report and analysis to those who were not present, so that the music or the performance has substantially the same meaning for them, so far as that is possible, that it had for those who attended. It is not to be expected that all who listened to a given musical program will agree with the critic. It is not even to be expected that all critics will agree. But it is to be assumed that where opinions are at odds, the reason for this divergence of views will be

found in individual constructions and personal preferences, with the basic facts reflected as substantially the
same.

Thus, it is quite understandable that one review should
be unfavorable, in this manner:

> Although the work exhibited no mean order of craftsmanship,
> the commonplace character of the themes gave to the composi-
> tion the dullness of mediocrity.

whereas, a second review, in substantial agreement with
the first as to the facts, should be favorable, as:

> Commonplace as were the themes, craftsmanship of no mean
> order redeemed the work from the dullness of mediocrity.

The mirror has intensified the same chief characteristics of the work in each instance, (a) the commonplace
themes and (b) the admirable craftsmanship, but the
reaction of the two reviewers has been antithetical as to
the worth of the composition. It is the reader's privilege
to disagree quite as heartily with any or all of the reviews he reads. But if what he reads clarifies and inten-
sifies for him the essentials on which opinion must be
based, the circumstance that such disagreement exists
does not take from the review its measure of value to
that particular reader. The critic, presumably, is an ex-
pert in listening; he has trained his faculties to seek out
the essentials; his is an active rather than a passive form
of audition; his mind goes forth to meet the music,
whereas it is only fair to say that the listener whose pur-

pose is that of an evening of musical pleasure, sits back expecting to have the music prod and stir his emotions. If it is not to be taken for granted that the critic is the only one listening for the sake of analysis, that is merely to admit there are many more critics in an audience than those who write for newspapers. It is to be believed that long training and diligent application *do* enable the critic to cleave to the reasons for the stir or the lack of stir, in a manner and to a degree not true of the generality of listeners with no such compulsion upon them. For them, it is enough to like, or not to like. If the critic can go no further than they, in dealing with the musical facts that underlie even the most divergent opinions, his mirror is not a very discerning one.

If this theory of criticism seems to reduce reviewing to a species of reporting, plus opinion, the author can only reply that in the day-to-day practice of newspaper writing, this is precisely what criticism is. Occasions arise in which analysis can be separated from news facts and even from opinion, as in the more extended discussions that are customarily to be found in the Sunday music pages. Even here, however, the element of timeliness tends to link these discussions to journalistic facts. Where criticism ends and musicology begins, how criticism may be coupled with propaganda for the advancement of a particular cause, when analysis becomes something of education rather than contemporary report, all the extensions of the critical function which tend to make the magazine article, the brochure, the biographical commentary and the programmatic ex-

egesis different from the daily newspaper review, involve
particular considerations that in no way invalidate what
has been set forth above. The medium determines the
variations. But the mirror function remains.

One mistaken view of criticism, prevalent among artists, is that its purpose is to enable them to fulfill their
destiny, as they see that destiny, in their chosen careers.
Criticism is for the *reader* and, ordinarily, for the artist
only to the extent that the artist may also be a reader.
If faults are enumerated, the reason for their enumeration ordinarily is not that the artist may be conscious of
them, but that the reflection of the mirror may be an adequate one for the reader. If virtues are detailed, this is
not primarily a form of commendation for the artist
but, like the enumeration of faults, an essential part of
the picture as passed on to the reader. There is a distinct
difference between the fault-finding of a teacher and
the fault-finding of a critic. The teacher has the duty of
correcting his pupil and of preparing him for a more
successful career. Criticism is not concerned with careers
or the preparation for them. It deals with the event, and
is only very slightly concerned (and then only by an extension of its true function) with what has not yet trans-
pired. If what the critic writes aids an artist to overcome
his faults and capitalize his good points, well and good.
But that is a corollary, a concomitant, a by-product, an
incidental service, and not the one the employer of the
critic had in mind when he assigned him to the duty of
reviewing music and the performances of musical artists.

The singer who has developed "holes" in the compass

may regard as bad criticism the review which points this out but makes no reference to a way of remedying the defect. The singer is wrong. She should go to a singing teacher. She cannot expect the critic to serve in that capacity. The violinist who plays out-of-tune has no complaint if the critic says so, without so much as a surmise as to whether it is a matter of faulty technique or a faulty ear. The pianist who blurs passages can expect to have his pedalling criticized without learning in print just what he is to do to clarify the passages that are confused. The conductor whose interpretations lack the intangible qualities of poetry and imagination need not feel aggrieved if he is given no clue as to how he is to set about acquiring these qualities. If the mirror has done its duty—if it has pictured the essentials as they were, at the particular performance in question—if the reader, listener or absentee, can grasp those essentials from reading the review—there has been no miscarriage of criticism. It has fulfilled its mission, irrespective of the manner in which the artist may have·been left at sea as to what he is to do about it.

Man to man, the critic may be able to advise him, but the mere fact that he is a discerning critic does not validate his advice. He is a fact-finder, not a miracle worker or even a good repair man. The singing teacher is the person to whom the singer should go when there is need of help. The violin pedagogue or the piano master should be the one to straighten out the troubles of the instrumentalist in need of specialized aid. The conductor and composer may profit from their fellows. No critic is to be presumed to know more about singing than singing teachers, more about the piano than piano teachers, more about the violin than violin teachers, or more about the technique of conducting and the art of composition than the men who have devoted their lives to the acquirement of mastery in these particular crafts. The critic has no such function of super-teacher as is assumed by artists when they talk of "constructive criticism", a term they construe to mean a kind of criticism that will enable them to better themselves, either as to their art or their place in the profession.

The only constructive criticism is good criticism. The only destructive criticism is bad criticism. And good and bad, in this connection, have nothing to do with whether the artist is helped along or set back. Criticism is good or bad according to whether the mirror, charged with the duty of reflecting the essentials, has done so, well or ill. A myriad of sidelights may interfere with that reflection, not the least of them the idiosyncrasies of the man in whose hands the mirror has been placed; but that only corroborates what has just been said. If these sidelights distort or misrepresent, the reflection is a bad one. All the good will in the world will not make a criticism constructive if it does not tell the truth.

Propaganda is no part of criticism. The critic who becomes the champion of a composer or an artist may be a public servant; he may advance the art he loves. But he does so in another capacity. And he does so, to his peril as a critic. He may be more useful if he ceases to be impartial. But he has sacrificed, for the time being, a

fundamental of his code. Of course, it is possible to be
both critic and propagandist. There are few single track
lives. With due dexterity, collisions may be avoided.
Double service may be achieved thereby. But always and
ever the reviewer who girds up his loins as a fighter in
behalf of any cause, other than that of the highest standards of the art, has need to remember that differences of
opinion about that cause may place him in the light of
being unfair to a rival cause. It is no new thing in the
history of art for the critic who espouses a Brahms to
set himself too radically against a Wagner. We cannot
well scold the Mahlerists or the Brucknerites for cam-
paigning in behalf of their respective idols, if we are to
place ourselves in the same position with respect to
Sibelius,* Strauss or Schönberg. Let us not say that the
critic should utterly eschew opportunities for service,
as he sees them, in this role of intermediary and thurifer.
But let us recognize the duality of his activities, whenever he associates himself with any movement savoring
of propaganda, and separate at once that part of his
labors, however valuable they may be, from his proper
functioning as a critical mirror. On occasion, the red-
blooded reviewer, impelled by reasons that to him are
too convincing to be denied, may forsake the too qui-
escent role of spectator and commentator for that of a
belligerent and apostle, and feel that he is serving a
higher function—but not that of criticism.

---

* An instance in which valuable and needed service has been done in
legitimate critical exegesis is found in various articles on Sibelius by Olin
Downes, critic for *The New York Times*.

THE CRITIC'S RESPONSIBILITIES

In the order named, the critic has responsibilities to the art of music, to himself, his readers, his employers and those he writes about. Much of the hostility, concealed or avowed, that exists between artists and critics is to be attributed to the mistaken notion of the artist that it is primarily for the artist that the critic has his being. So small, relatively, is the responsibility of the critic to the artist, as distinct from the art which both the artist and the critic seek to serve, that it has been contended, and with sound reason so far as the actual practice of the profession is involved, that the artist is not properly one of the critic's considerations in his effort to fulfil his mission and live up to his code.

Let us consider here the words of Lawrence Gilman:*

The chief aim of a newspaper critic must be to interest the general reader. And if he can interest those readers who have not heard the performance, as well as those who have, he is entitled to call it a day. Quite apart from its value as a report and estimate of a musical performance, his criticism must be able to stand alone as an interesting, readable story. . . .

---

* Lawrence Gilman, music critic of the *New York Herald Tribune* and author of the program annotations for the New York Philharmonic-Symphony. Quoted from an interview in Editor & Publisher.

The music critic should never forget that his chief concern
is with the reader, not with the artist he may happen to be discussing. . . . I have learned never to think of the probable
effect of my comments on the performers who may be involved.
That would be a disastrous pre-occupation. From the point of
view of the critic, the interests of the performer do not enter
into the matter at all.

As already emphasized in the chapter devoted to the
function of criticism, the critic is not a super-teacher. It
is not for him to tell the artist how to overcome faults.
It is for him to point out that the faults exist. The latter
is an essential of his function as a mirror, to enable the
reader to see, in words, what the trained ear has heard
in sounds. The mirror is not a studio. It does not con-
duct master-classes. The teaching profession is something else. To that profession should be left the repair
work or the advanced study that is needed in particular
instances. The reader, for whom the mirror functions, is
not concerned with this. The artist may also be a reader,
but the review was not written for his benefit. He comes
into the picture only incidentally. And it is only incidentally that the critic has an obligation to him. His
obligation to himself imposes upon him all the fairness,
the courtesy, the seriousness that the artist can ask of
him. His readers and his employers require it of him.
He can scarcely be true to his conceptions of the art if
he permits himself to be led away from fairness by personal bias or a desire to be scintillantly cruel at the artist's expense. It can thus be shown that all the critic
owes to the artist is already a part of what he owes to

the art, to himself, to his readers and to his employer.

The rub comes when the circumstances require the critic to fulfil one or the other of these obligations in a manner the artist regards as injurious to his reputation or his career. But the critic who has either to present an incomplete and misleading reflection, or to injure an artist's reputation and career, is in duty bound to disregard the latter consideration. As Mr. Gilman has said, this is not legitimately the critic's concern, however much the artist may persist in regarding criticism as something which either helps or hinders in the achievement of the success which is the artist's goal.

Reduced to its essential, a position of this kind is almost certain to appear more drastic when put into words than it actually works out to be in day-to-day critical practice. The ordinary humanity of ordinary human beings, in or out of the profession, often results in suggestions which may prove helpful to the artist. There is reason to feel, however, that in the main the mirror function is preserved and that most of what is written about an artist serves its purpose primarily as an informative report and analysis for the disinterested reader.

In placing the critic's first responsibility to the art, it may be assumed that we have put a brake upon his own egoism and the desire to exploit his own gifts; things he may share, quite naturally, with the most self-assertive artist. If he is conscious of this first obligation, he may acquire a reasonable humility and self-effacement, beyond which it is scarcely to be expected that he can go and still assert something of personality in his writing. Reverence need not be of a painfully pious order to serve as a safeguard against pin-sticking and petty wise-cracking. There is no place for the sadistic in a true love of music. To serve the art earnestly is to cultivate the sympathies rather than to stifle them. The more exacting and well-informed the criticism, the less it will tend to the superficialities of clever satire. What this responsibility to the art can mean may be brought home to us by reflection on the immeasurable influence of the writings of one man, the veteran W. J. Henderson * who, in the opinion of the author of this book, has done more to elevate standards in America than any single figure that can be named among either executive or educative musicians.

The critic's responsibilities to himself are those of conscience. He cannot meet them if he is slack or careless or easily turned aside, much less dishonest, in his opinions. He cannot fulfil them if he rests content, at any stage of his career, with his own knowledge and equipment. He can never regard the task of preparation as over and done. He must go on to the end, enlarging his experience, supplementing his background, dilating his spirit to take in the changes of the times. Eternal study is imposed upon him.

To his employer, the critic owes the sort of dependable service that meets the requirements of his particular field and those of the particular medium for which he

---

* W. J. Henderson, music critic of the *New York Sun*. He is the Dean of New York's critics.

writes. It is not for him to exalt himself, if that should be possible, by a species of writing that is contrary to the style and purposes of the publication. If the medium is wrong for him, he should find another medium. But no employer can rightfully ask of a critic that he repress or misrepresent the opinions necessary to the truthfulness of his review. Style is adaptable. Judgments are not.

The critic's responsibilities to his readers constitute the major part of his cares, from day to day. It is of them he thinks when he pens or types his review. It is for them that he chooses his words, his illustrations, his metaphors, his array of facts in support or elucidation of his opinions. If he does his full duty by them he will have served the art, he will have been true to himself, he will have met his obligations to his employer. His full duty done, he may find that he has ruffled the pride, perhaps even diminished the earnings of the artist. To regret this is to be human, but his service to the art is not to be measured by the degree or the multiplicity of such regrets.

BOOK TWO

THE APPRAISAL OF MUSIC

AN APPROACH TO A METHOD

To M. D. Calvocoressi * immediate acknowledgment must be made for the skeletal basis of this and succeeding chapters devoted to the critical approach to music, and more particularly new music. In his admirable little volume on Musical Criticism, published some ten years ago, he may be said to have evolved a method that has at least the color of science. Like so many other methods, it is a rationalization of procedure already in vogue; a reduction to its essentials of a practice somewhat confused by the vagaries of those concerned with it; a recognition and definition of the workings of criticism, after the fact. Consciously or unconsciously, critics have been following the lines of thought and action traced by Calvocoressi. He has held up the mirror to them, as they have striven to hold up the mirror to the music they have been called upon to criticize. By intensifying the essentials and virtually eliminating the unessentials, he has supplied a book on the larger aspects of criticism that achieves substantially the sort of reflection the critic aims at in the evaluation of compositions and perform-

---

* M. D. Calvocoressi, distinguished Greek-French critic, lecturer and author.

ances. It is a book of theory. The aim of this volume is one more pragmatic, more specifically concerned with practice. Student and professional critic alike can profit by earnest consideration of Calvocoressi's seasoned study of fundamentals. His book is one strongly to be recommended.

Though it is true that in practice the larger part of a daily newspaper critic's writing is devoted to performance, the more important aspects of his work are those that have to do with the appraisal of music. What he writes about the older music, already established, may be interesting and informative. It may even play a part in righting some injustices of long-standing. But this, again, is secondary to his consideration of new or otherwise unfamiliar compositions. It is with respect to these that his readers will have most need for guidance: the intensification of essentials and elimination of unessentials, the unbiased analysis that will distinguish between matter and manner, substance and fashion, material and method, message and technical gloss, the end achieved and the theoretical considerations involved. Much keener powers of perception are required to form a first judgment of music never before experienced, particularly if it be in an advanced idiom, than to confirm or dispute what others have thought out in coping with music already rated as good, bad or mediocre. Confronted with new music, many listeners throw up their hands. They are uncertain as to what they do think about it. They are nonplussed, confused, the essentials escape them. Sonorities may impress them, without their having any very definite feeling as to the quality of the thematic material or the nature of the structure. Or they may be repelled by dissonances, by the length, the violence or the placidity of a work. They may be repelled and attracted at the same time; wearied through two-thirds of a composition, only to be briskly stimulated by a brilliant close.

The critic's business is to cleave through the obscurities and contrary leadings of a composition to those basic considerations which will enable him to know where he stands. If he trusts only his sensory reactions, he will be little better off than those for whom it is his duty to write intelligently and to some clear purpose. He must work as he listens. He must think things out. In the place of unordered reactions, he must have something resembling a method. Every sound critic has one, though he may never have reasoned it out the way Calvocoressi has. There *are* standards and there are ways of *applying* standards. And though difference of opinion may result, there is probably a much larger agreement among critics concerning these standards and their application than either the writers themselves or their readers ever realize.

As enucleated by Calvocoressi, three main considerations enter into criticism and determine what the critic thinks and writes. The first of these is the *critic himself,* his predispositions, biases, likes and dislikes, temperament, mode of thought, knowledge, experience, musicality, all that can be summed up as the man and his background. The second is *the direct data* for appraisal, supplied by the music itself, its thematic and harmonic substance, its rhythmic character, its style and workmanship; the data of its printed or manuscript page and the data of the sound it makes when performed. The third is *the indirect data,* which come, not from the music itself, but from many correlated sources, such as the "program" the composer may have used as his literary subject matter; all disclosures made by the composer or by another as to his aims and intentions; all information derived from other compositions by the same composer or those of his particular school; all biographical and other information derived from books, annotations, discussions; everything, in fact, which tends to shed a light on a composition but which does not proceed from the actual notation on paper or the sound in performance.

These three considerations, then, govern appraisal. Accepting the critic as he is, his ability, temperament, equipment and experience, the first of the three considerations may be reduced, for the purpose of discussion of an approach to a method, to his *predispositions.* They need to be considered as consciously as the *direct data* and the *indirect data.* They will be discussed here as one of the important factors in that mental attitude by which the critic goes out to meet the music, rather than sitting back to let the music come to him. They will be regarded as sharpening or dulling the fine edge of the scalpel he applies in getting under the skin of the music he hears. The critic will make it a point to know himself, to know the music and to know all he can know of facts surrounding the music and the man who wrote the music. Brought together, *predispositions, direct data* and *indirect data,* determine what he thinks. If he has learned to write, he may then achieve the difficult task of writing what he thinks. If he does, his mirror has done its job.

THE CRITIC'S PREDISPOSITIONS

In conducting a class in professional criticism at the Curtis Institute, the author found in his students biases that would have been handicaps in the practice of the profession. These were advanced music students, several majoring in composition. They were well equipped in technical knowledge, though limited in experience. Several had built their faith so solidly on "pure" music as to be impatient with music of a programmatic character. One, devoutly attached to Bach, was free to confess a distaste for all eighteenth century music. Others could see no virtue in atonality; for them it violated fundamental laws, though whether those laws were acoustical, mathematical, God-given or man-made no one was quite prepared to say. These biases were so diverse in character as to react differently in each individual's case, for or against different music, but for each they would have militated in some degree against an open mind, an open heart and an open ear. If this could be true of advanced students, keenly concerned with the practice of a living, changing art, how inevitable that such biases should be prevalent among laymen, including journalists for whom music is a secondary interest, as music undoubt-

edly is for many who practice criticism only incidentally
to some other form of newspaper work. The man who
knows what he likes, and listens to hear just that, be he
musician, layman or journalist, or any other combina-
tion thereof, is likely to hold up a very undependable
mirror when he comes to passing on a reflection of what
he has heard.

Inevitably, something of this intrudes upon all professional criticism. But it is guided and guarded. Casual
conversations between critics will bring to light preferences for one type of music or another, sometimes as
distinct as the preferences of laymen. In contradistinc-
tion to the student who had little sympathy for any
eighteenth century music, a critic might be heard to
confess to his colleague that his personal god was Mozart. If he had his choice of "Così fan Tutte" at one
opera house, conducted by Richard Strauss, and Wagner's "Tristan und Isolde" at another, conducted by
Toscanini, he would go to "Così fan Tutte". Not so
much because he considered the Mozart work the more
divinely inspired but because it gave him greater personal joy. The other might agree, and then, to the
amazement of any third person listening, say: "But not
if the Wagner work were 'Siegfried' ". For the critic
who spoke first, "Tristan" might mean much more than
"Siegfried". The discussion might lead into some still
more surprising confidence as to a veritable passion for
Smetana's "Bartered Bride" and only professional respect for "Parsifal". "Don Giovanni" might be riddled
on one hand and acclaimed on the other. At the bottom

of all this would be found personal attraction or absence of attraction, with a good deal of substantial agreement on the points that would enter into a critical appraisal of these works.

Calvocoressi, adapting a proposal made by J. M. Robert in his "New Essays toward a Critical Method" (literary criticism rather than music criticism) suggests that the critic or prospective critic draw up a credo or confession of biases, setting forth on paper that he has a leaning toward this, that and the other, and feels an aversion for the other, that and this; thus enumerating for his own benefit his likes and dislikes, his sympathies and antipathies; his predilections for, and his predispositions against. He does not recommend that the critic thrust any such confession on his readers. Rather, the critic will strive not to do so unconsciously in his writings; certain as these are to reflect his special enthusiasms, and, perhaps in less degree, his coolness or aversion where enthusiasm is not for him. Students of the course in criticism under the author's direction at the Curtis Institute found this confession a difficult matter. When they came to analyzing their own inclinations, some could discover only that they liked what was "good" and disliked what was "bad". They had difficulty in identifying any positive biases. But ordinary class-room discussion developed these biases in a very respectable number. Some, obviously, were based on *indirect data;* on what the students had read about certain works or composers or periods of composition, rather than on their personal experience; some were the result of their own efforts in composition and of what they had been taught in the struggle for self-realization; others, such as one in which the student said that "music in the raw", i.e., folk music, was not music to him, and became music only when it was transformed by an artist into an expression of that artist's musical personality, were clearly the result of associations. A student who was certain he had no predispositions, hence felt unable to write any confession of any kind, could scarcely be induced to hear or write about any music that involved the human voice. He shared the feeling of many instrumentalists that singing is not music.

Exceptional, indeed, the critic who can look back over as many as ten years of actual practice in his profession and find nothing there to support a contention that predispositions plague us all. Berlioz, a keen critic in spite of some flamboyant characteristics, had scant sympathy for chromaticism. For him the "Tristan" Prelude was wearisome and distasteful, a "kind of chromatic wail". Let another confess that in his boyhood he was puzzled at having to learn to like "Tristan", whereas he was swept away by his first "Meistersinger". It was not until he began to note that parts of "Parsifal" and "Tannhäuser" tired him in the same way that "Tristan" did, that he decided the secret was a physical one, in some way related to his sensory reaction to chromaticism. The diatonic "Meistersinger" had no such hurdle to surmount. The question was not one of mental recognition of the supreme qualities in each of these works. It was one of physical comfort in the diatonic and physical discomfort in the chromatic. The only cure was the hearing of much chromatic music, until finally the notion that the diatonic was natural and sympathetic, the chromatic labored and fatiguing, was completely worn away.

Undoubtedly many individuals have a similar feeling for the tonal and against the atonal. They find sunlight and the normal emotions in works adhering to the key system; they find abnormality and a great weariness in compositions which abjure that system. How much of this is purely physical, how much is association, how much is the smugness of those who do not want to be disturbed by innovations that run contrary to their accepted ideas and their previous experience, is not for this volume to undertake to decide.

Preconceptions as to what music *should be,* have ever been stumbling blocks to fair listening and just criticism. The new is chaotic because it does not conform to the old. It lacks melody because its melody is cast in an unfamiliar mold. It is harsh because its accents and its harmonic devices are not the pre-digested ones of the elder era. All musical affection is based in some degree on recognition, which implies reminiscence in a majority of instances. The music that is loved is familiar music, the music that is in the blood. In most instances, new music can hope for a similar love only when it also has become familiar, when it also is in the blood. That is why a succeeding generation venerates what often was received with doubt and controversy when it was new. There were preconceptions to overcome. There were affections to be built through familiarity. Only with a

little time could these flower in the blood. All this assumes, of course, that we are dealing with music worthy
of living on.

How to avoid or at least minimize his preconceptions
at the same time that he develops and applies his standards is the problem of the critic. From the mistakes of
the past, he learns certain cautions that help him to prevent his criteria from so hardening as to be applicable
only to what conforms to the models bequeathed from
an earlier time. His standards may involve considerations that are timeless; he may believe that they will be
just as applicable a decade hence as they were last year;
but he will feel the need for flexibility and fluidity in
their application, knowing that nothing is changeless
but change. In guarding against preconceptions, he will
take due consideration of predispositions, realizing that
these may not be the product of thought or of standards,
but of emotional or physical reactions, and of associations that interact upon his feelings. He will not try to
obliterate these predispositions, for *through* them will
come much of his own pleasure in music and, perhaps,
the ability to go further than his fellows in the explora-
tion of some particular field—a field in which he may
excel as a specialist, an authority. But he will strive to
be eternally conscious of them, so that he will be their
master, not their slave. He will dominate them, they will
not dominate him. He will guide them, not be guided
by them.

As a minor instance of what is involved, it is said that
public school music teachers found in the youth of the

period which immediately followed the World War a distaste for three-four time, amounting almost to an inability to grasp the rhythmic pulse of the old-fashioned waltz. The jerky jazz rhythm had alienated sympathy for music that possessed a gliding grace. Of opposite predilections were lovers of the Vienna waltzes, who could feel no sympathy for jazz. One of the latter group, if given responsibility, might approach a jazz concerto with a distaste he knew was likely to influence him adversely in the writing of his review. Knowledge of his own bias was half the battle. The one way for him to be fair was to subject his adverse reactions to a species of critical cross-examination. With every word of unfavorable comment he felt called upon to write, it was his duty to ask himself whether, if this had been a Vienna waltz, perhaps equally "popular" in character and no more resourceful in workmanship, he would have felt as antagonistic to it. Was he criticising the particular composition or was he condemning the type? Was he applying standards or was he confessing to his readers a predisposition that was dictating to him?

But doesn't this sort of self-discipline put the critic's feelings in a strait-jacket? Doesn't it take away the joy of listening? Even if the answer were "yes"—and the author's personal experience tells him it must be "no"—the governing fact would be that the critic's function is not that of enjoyment but of doing to the best of his ability the work he is employed to do.

DIRECT DATA—THE MUSIC

Leaning frankly on Mr. Calvocoressi once more, let us consider next the question of *direct data*. This is the data we derive from the music itself. Theoretically, nothing of a literary or a programmatic nature enters into it; nothing historical, nothing biographical, nothing of personal avowal of aims and purposes. Practically, it may well be that few of the critical fraternity ever take due note of craftsmanship without something of the historical being involved. It may not be possible even to weigh the question of the freshness or the banality of material without some extra-musical consideration influencing the evaluation, as will be discussed further in a separate section devoted to the subject of banality. The fitness of music for its purpose often is an issue.

Of all considerations entering into criticism, no other has the importance of the data derived from the music itself. If music were always what the pundits style "pure music", it might be possible to eliminate all other considerations, though the writer cannot help feeling that if the historical sense were discounted to this extent, so that the associations of various periods and world trends were made negligible, art and humanity would be immeasurably the losers. The issue of program music will be touched upon further in a succeeding section.

Direct data from the music may be resolved into three principal contributory factors. The first is the material: melodic, rhythmic, harmonic. The second is the form, in some instances easily separable, in other instances inextricably bound up with the material. The third is the workmanship, again in varying degree severable, in any critical analysis of a composition, from the material and the form. The writer has heard students stoutly contend that they could not consider material apart from form and workmanship. No doubt their contention would be difficult to reason out of court in the case of many highly organized art works, in which every element seems to have sprung simultaneously and with the same inevitability from the composer's brain. But certainly, Beethoven's use of a Russian air in one of his Rasoumovsky quartets, and Moussorgsky's use of that same air in his music-drama, "Boris Godounoff"—neither merely an example of folk-tune harmonization—make it clear that the same material can be used for different forms; and the existence of that air independent of these forms can be regarded as sufficient to show that material, form and workmanship are, indeed, separable things.

One of the first things any one writing about music has to learn is that there are too many kinds of music in a world that can make room at one and the same time for a Palestrina motet, a Bach fugue, a Mozart serenade, a Beethoven sonata, a Schubert Lied, a Brahms symphony, a Wagner music-drama, a Strauss tone-poem and a Stravinsky ballet, for the application of any such theory as one of form governing material or material determining form. What is true of *much* music is untrue of *some* music. Criticism must deal with all music and on its own terms.

Eventually, most critics undoubtedly come to think of *material* first. Not all, but most of what is sheer genius in music, as distinct from what is artistry or mastery, gets back to material. Would one say, then, that the unknown originator of a beautiful folk-tune had more genius than the superb craftsman who utilized that tune? Undoubtedly, there are instances in which the answer could be in the affirmative; though it is possible to believe that in the instance of one such tune coming into the mind of a simple peasant and being bequeathed by him to posterity, there was more of accident than of genius in his hitting upon this succession of notes, with their rhythms and their time values. The melody may have the quality of genius; but the genius that is confined to the production of one unharmonized tune may have been no genius at all. The importance of many such melodies lies in what may be done with them— either literally or in some re-distillation which may be a matter of racial inheritance rather than any conscious adaptation or imitation—by the artist with an art purpose.

In thinking first of material, the critic is fortified by the lessons to be learned from the entire past of music. Much music has been important to its own time because of its manner or details of its workmanship, only to fall by the wayside thereafter because the material was not of the quality to command admiration after the manner was no longer the vogue and when advances of technique had made commonplace the once admired workmanship. Other music has lived on because of the power and beauty of the material, when manner and workmanship came to be recognized as outdated.

A likeness may be drawn to the charm of an individual and the influence of dress. A beautiful woman in an old photograph may be beautiful in spite of her attire. The fashion that caused her to be much admired in her time may become her not at all in the eyes of a subsequent generation. Another woman even more strikingly dressed for her day, may have been much admired in that era by reason of her elegant appearance. After thirty years, the features are found to be plain. The once fashionable garments are now a little grotesque. Style cannot play the part for the subsequent generation that it did for its own day. One face is beautiful in spite of the dress. The plainness of the other is made the plainer thereby. We may view the material of the music as the face, the musical manner as the style in attire. Many a lesser composer wrote in the manner of Mozart. The manner alone could not keep his music current. It is a defunct manner, today. But the material that Mozart created—the equivalent of the beautiful face—has placed him for all time among the greatest melodists and the greatest composers.

The critic, then, often delves for the material as his first consideration. He is wary of musical fashions, wary of manners, wary of those devices which are of a particular time, knowing that they may tend to mislead him as to the worth of the material. He may have difficulty separating material from manner, and, more particularly, material from form. But he will make the effort, to satisfy himself so far as this may be possible as to the quality of the material as material. He knows from experience that there will be times when, as W. J. Henderson has said (of the Strauss "Elektra") he will have reason to "suspect that a measurable amount of poor drawing is carefully disguised in very splendid paint".

With respect to material, the critic has to determine, if he can, whether it is spontaneous or labored, fresh or trite, personal or reminiscent, refined or vulgar, stimulating or banal—all that enters into what we term inspiration, as against a lack of inspiration. Inevitably also, he must determine its serviceableness for the uses to which it is put, which will mean that it must be considered, not for itself alone, but in the light of its relation to the form; and its expressiveness in realizing the composer's intent—a consideration that frequently will be found to couple the *direct data* of the music with the *indirect data* of a program or other extra-musical factor.

Whatever may be argued with respect to the limitations that are imposed upon the creation of original material, the fact remains that in most of the music that has outlived its own era the material has retained an impressive originality, personality or individuality. The lesser composer may have reason to complain that it is not just to describe his music as sounding like that of

Brahms, Wagner, Debussy, Strauss or Stravinsky. But
this sort of criticism, tiresome though it is, goes straight
to the heart of things. Brahms, Wagner, Debussy,
Strauss and Stravinsky do not have to be described as
sounding like some one else.

In considering material first, the critic will be conscious of rhythmic and harmonic personality as well as
of melodic personality. But he may prefer to think of
details of orchestration, in the case of a symphonic work,
as a matter of workmanship rather than material, granting that it may be quite as indicative of what is personal
in the composer's creation. Mozart said of himself that
he orchestrated simultaneously with the thematic creation; that he heard the complete scoring of an idea in
the same instant that the idea had its birth. But it remains possible to conceive of those ideas as orchestrated
otherwise. We know that a similar genius in the creation
of melodic material, Schubert, thought first in terms of
melody, then approached the task of orchestration separately. There are sketches for the entire third movement of the "Unfinished" Symphony. Schubert wrote
out the melodic line completely. But he orchestrated
only a few bars on the uncompleted page of the manuscript sent to the Graz Musical Society. (Not as has
been erroneously stated so many times, composed *for*
that society.)

This apparently opposite approach does not make it
any the less possible to judge Mozart's melodic creation
and his orchestration separately, as is done with the
melodic creation and the orchestration of Schubert.

The critic who is a stickler for form is likely to find himself on dangerous ground. His critical purpose is not to prescribe form, but to recognize it, so that he will understand the structure of a composition. Without that understanding, his mirror may not pass on a clear reflection. To insist that a symphony is *not* a symphony because it is not in conformity with a standardized pattern is perilous; since, from the first, the symphony has been in a state of flux. Beethoven's substitution of the Scherzo for the Minuet was a departure as contrary to existing form as any of the later developments which have occasioned controversy among formalists. If one were to accept the contentions of Cecil Gray in his Sibelius biography, Schubert, Schumann, Brahms, and in fact virtually all who have written symphonies since Beethoven, wrote not symphonies but something else. His contention is that the nineteenth century Germans were misled by the Lied. Instead of using themes as building blocks for their symphonic structure, they stretched and adapted the structure so as to incorporate material that was not of itself symphonic; with the result that their form ceased to be the symphonic form. It is largely on this basis that Mr. Gray contends that Sibelius is the greatest master of the symphony since Beethoven. The others, including Brahms, are conveniently pigeon-holed somewhere else.

But the critic, as we have said, is concerned with all types of music. It is not his purpose to take from the world any of the pleasure and the consolation that have been brought into it by men of genius, whatever the form in which they wrote. If he turns from Mr. Gray's "Sibelius", to Gabriel Engel's "Mahler", he will find Mahler acclaimed as "the song symphonist". On the one hand, Brahms was no symphonist because he was led away by song. On the other hand, Mahler was a great symphonist because he was addicted to song. The critic will do well to leave such hair-splitting to propagandists and partisans, the while he takes due note of the nature of the form of a specific work, to the end that he can analyze and describe it, and reach some conclusion as to its effectiveness; but not with intent to resist any extension or modification that may add to the variety, the scope, the expressiveness and the appeal of the art of music. He will be the last to deny that there is beauty in design. He will know that much of the strength of great music is in its architecture. But he will be wise to conclude that labels are one thing, design or architecture another. The worth of music will never be determined by the strictness with which it conforms to a classification. But for Bach, we might not be aware today that there are so many different kinds of fugues.

Form, free or strict, implies a cohesion and a coherence that are of immediate concern to the reviewer. The work that justifies itself in this respect will have form, whether it be called a sonata or a rhapsody. The critic's business is to see that his mirror does not reflect the rhapsody as being in effect a sonata; which is not quite the same thing as averring that though Brahms was a great composer he was not a great symphonist because of his predilection for the Lied. The practiced reviewer senses awkward construction in music as the practiced literary reader senses awkward construction in verse or prose. Clumsy structure can be noted in the hearing, as well as from study of the printed page. Design, too, can be cut and dried. Though much wine is poured into old bottles, most of the important composers have had to have bottles of their own. The general shape may have been the same; but we know a Mozart bottle could not have held the Beethoven wine, any more than a Haydn bottle could have held the Brahms wine. Let the reviewer, therefore, think of form as a medium, rather than as a container, and see his own function in relation to form as the duty to describe, not to prescribe or proscribe.

It has been said that the critic will be wary of manner, as manner may be merely the fashion of the day. He will realize, however, that every composer will reflect his era. Moreover, he will often find, in what may be summed up as manner, the badge of a composer's individuality. This manner will be important if it is fundamental with the man, rather than something extraneous by which the artist has made himself representative of his time. Puccini was a mannerist. He was typical of his day. But his musical personality was in his manner. There was no sham about him, no affectation. He wrote *his* way. It is not our purpose to pass judgment on individual composers, or in any way seek to shape the opinions of those who may consult this book. But Puccini may be pondered, along with Massenet and others of an era that is not the era of today, as raising a question as to whether the material of this music is important enough to survive successive changes of manner or fashion. Where, today, are the operas of Salieri, a favorite of Mozart's day? Where those of Méhul? Of Marschner? Each of these represented a manner that had its day and came back no more.

Craftsmanship comes properly within the sphere of *direct data*. From the music itself, either in the hearing or in study of the printed page, the skill with which a composer has achieved his ends is to be determined. The ear-test, ordinarily is the better one. What is written on paper is of small consequence if it does not come off, if it does not "sound". But there can be no doubt that sometimes what the eye discovers contributes to quick recognition by the ear of some particularly deft achievement, which otherwise would reveal itself at the fifth or tenth hearing rather than the first. We may assume by craftsmanship all that pertains to the composer's handling of his material and particularly its adaptation for the musical resources to be employed in its performance.

Since the time of Berlioz, orchestration has become a subject the critic is never likely to exhaust. Always there will be more to learn. But he will need to be on his guard against giving anything like the same importance to beauty of scoring that he would give to beauty of material or even beauty of form. Scoring is much more a matter of the day, much more a thing of fashion, much more a praxis of temporary technique. The great themes of Beethoven are as remarkable today as when they first were sounded. The effects by which Berlioz amazed contemporaries and so strongly influenced Liszt and Wagner (who in turn opened the doors for Strauss) have been materially tamed by the advances of the very men he put to work. Today, it is the rule rather than the exception to orchestrate well. But to orchestrate individually is another matter, whether in the traditional manner or the newer fashions of the post-war modernists. It is for the critic to determine not merely whether a composer has orchestrated well, but whether he has orchestrated with a set of stencils and generous use of a rubber stamp.

INDIRECT DATA—FROM SOURCES OTHER THAN THE MUSIC

The critic who knew nothing whatever about the composer of the music he was called upon to evaluate, nothing of his aims and purposes and nothing of any extra-musical consideration involved, might form a very fair judgment so far as basic worth of material and skill of craftsmanship were at stake, and still make some serious blunder that would vitiate this judgment. The layman, less experienced than he in tracking down the essentials of what is called "pure" music, might avoid the same mistake by reason of some special knowledge of the composer or of the composition which the critic did not possess. If there were only one kind of music, and this music the absolute music which is but a fraction of our total stock, there would be much less danger of reading into a work something that was not there, a mistake as open to the critic as to the layman. What we call *indirect data*—the data that are derived from sources other than the music itself—are primarily of value because they throw the necessary light on considerations the critic soon finds he cannot escape in dealing with music not of the absolute order. The tendency to invent meanings for music where no meaning is known, and to weave fictitious romances about compositions when the facts of their creation are obscure, is not to be evaded on the assumption that all such meanings and romancings are unnecessary. The one sure way to prevent false meanings and false facts being attributed to music is to ascertain the true ones and make them known.

As this is not a book of aesthetics, space will not be occupied here with argument over such theories as that of the necessity of knowing the man to understand his art, or of comprehending his times so as to see in his works the flowering of the *Zeitgeist*. A wide reading of such subjects is expected of the critic and to each individual must be left the formulation or adaptation of such aesthetic principles as he is convinced will have a direct bearing on his critical task. But his day-to-day writing will soon convince him of the necessity of knowing all he can know of biographical and similar data, for the practical purposes of journalism as well as for the clear-headedness of his own approach. The more he can constitute himself a walking program-annotation for whatever he hears, the less he will be harassed by doubts and disturbing cross-currents in his thinking and his writing.

There is no escaping the fact that the growth or the decline of a great figure in music comes within the ordinary scope of the writing of a music critic. To see in the later works of Richard Strauss a degree of sterility as compared to those of his middle life is not to stray from the ordinary purview of criticism. But to impute through ignorance of dates that same sterility to some early work, like the Serenade for Wind Instruments, written before Strauss had developed his own personality, as if it were a product of the period of his "Schlagobers" or his "Aegyptische Helena", would be to make the criticism ridiculous. Bare chronology, then, can have its importance, not merely with regard to the music of differing eras, but the music of a single composer. Mozart's boyhood "Bastien and Bastienne" may be no better music for having been written at the age of twelve, but to mistakenly assume that it followed "Don Giovanni" and "Magic Flute" would be to make preposterous whatever judgment was formed about it.

No doubt the question of the originality of a work is illumined by all possible knowledge of other and similar works of its own time. The composer of today who imitates Hindemith or Stravinsky might seem more original if we had no knowledge of Hindemith or Stravinsky. Yet this is as much a matter of *indirect data* as is knowledge of dates and eras. It does not come from the music itself, but from other music. Knowledge of this kind is a safeguard against assumptions that are assumptions of fact as well as matters of opinion. The critic soon finds that the interplay of fact and opinion colors and influences most of what he writes. The essential is that his facts be as extensive and as nearly right as he can make them.

The rub is that the lay listener is not the only one who invents mental programs that have nothing to do with the case. Biographers and authorities of every kind have perpetuated errors. Composers have devised sources of inspiration *after the fact* and have seen their aims and goals in the light of what their music turned out to be, or how it appealed to the public. But an error of judgment based upon this sort of error of fact is at least an enlightened error; as compared to the error of ignorance likely to be made by the man who does not concern himself with biographical, historical and other extra-musical considerations.

The more extended the critic can make the reading and the study that stock him with indirect data, the more checks he has on mis-statements likely to lead him into error. His research will guide him in many instances to the true fact behind the false one. Calvocoressi cites an instance of what uncorroborated acceptance of a composer's own statement of the origin of a composition may mean. Berlioz declared that the "Marche au Supplice" of the "Symphonie Fantastique" was written "during a night of fever", of which he spent the greater part roving through snow-clad fields while Chopin and Liszt sought his body at the Paris mortuary. The March, however, has been shown to have been transferred, with only the addition of four bars at the end, from an earlier work, "Les Francs-Juges", and while it may originally have been written in "a night of fever", any association with the "Fantastic" of a white heat of inspiration is scarcely justified on the basis of what Berlioz says about the March. The quality of the music is not altered by this knowledge of the history of the March. But the critic is safeguarded against some rash comparison of the spontaneity of this movement with that of the Scene in the Fields, which Berlioz said he composed slowly, with much difficulty and with many revisions.

As a second instance of how knowledge of the transference of music from one opus to another may safeguard a critic against an assumption which would begin with error of fact and end in unsound opinion, let us consider the scene of the prayer and the farewell of Boris to his son in Moussorgsky's music-drama, "Boris Godounoff". Much has been written of the mating in Moussorgsky's music of the note and the word. It has been contended in some quarters that he achieved what Wagner sought but did not achieve; that text and music, with Moussorgsky, are one and indisseverable, a union resulting in a form of musical speech wherein precise equivalents are merged. The scene named is one of the most effective, dramatically, musically and emotionally, in Moussorgsky's greatest work. It might well be cited, therefore, as an illustration of music that came into being as the tonal equivalent of the words. This would be a disastrous assumption. The critic's words would be made absurd by the knowledge—scarcely common property among those who admire and extoll "Boris Godounoff"—that the prayer of this scene was originally a Hymn to Moloch in Moussorgsky's earlier opera, "Salammbo", and was conceived without thought of the dying Boris and his adjurations to his son. Knowledge of this fact in no way lessens the beauty or the aptness of this music to the scene in which it was incorporated. But it protects the reviewer against some critical mistake, one which would be the result of knowing more, rather than less, than the layman, but of not knowing enough.

The issue of program music is one to be debated elsewhere than in the day-to-day criticisms of the reviewer holding up a mirror to what he has heard. His task is to write about the program music he hears, as he writes about the absolute music he hears. Program music is for him an established fact and he can no more ignore it than he can ignore the presence of an English horn in some symphonies—in the face of the assertion by Gounod (supported sympathetically by Cecil Gray) that the English horn is not properly an instrument of the symphonic ensemble. There are all manner of programs, vague or precise; some, mere titles for long movements or whole compositions not otherwise elucidated; some, prodigiously detailed scenarios like the one which listeners to the Strauss "Don Quixote" find all but impossible to carry in the head. The critic is forced to deal with these things as he finds them. It is well for him to know the program of "Don Quixote", if only not to speak of the windmill battle when the virtuosity he is commenting on has had to do with the supposed flight through the air on the steed that never left the ground. Whatever his own convictions on program music, he must deal with "Don Quixote" on its own terms, as he must deal with Debussy's "Afternoon of a Faun" or Stravinsky's "Rites of Spring" on theirs. He cannot deal with them as he would deal with Bach's "Art of Fugue".

Knowledge of the program of a work may not make any clearer whether it is good or bad music, but may prevent evaluating the work for something it is not. For one thing (and this, no doubt, has influenced composers), the frank avowal of a program serves to put a stop to the imagining of other programs, a common enough process, as anyone who discusses music with his neighbors or reads commentaries extensively is made aware of, day by day. Beethoven, in giving certain broad descriptions to the movements of his Sixth or "Pastoral" Symphony, saved that work from the welter of conflicting notions that have found their way into print as to the nature of the Seventh Symphony, ranging from "the spirit of the dance" to the tramp of armies. To know that the thunder of the "Pastoral" is only thunder, is to be protected against some assumption that here is a heartbreak over the immortal beloved. There are thunders, too, in the Strauss "Rosenkavalier". But the text and the stage action suffice to inform us that this is only the Straussian way of underlining a witticism or a bit of a prank. The thunderstorm of Rossini's "Barber of Seville" would almost qualify as a lullaby in some modern works. It would be neither better nor worse as music, but the critic who wrote admiringly of this thunderstorm as an example of Rossini's charm as a writer of lullabies could be exculpated only by proof positive that his tongue was in his cheek.

In considering a composer's avowal of his aims, the critic needs to be informed primarily as a safeguard against attributing some other aim to the man or his work. It is by no means imperative that the critic see the composition as the composer saw it. Whatever his pur-

poses, the composer may not have achieved them, or
they may not have been worth achieving. Or, contrari-
wise, the composer may have built better than he knew.
Nor is the critic required by his conscience to take it for
granted that the composer always knows what he is
talking about when he goes in for self-revelation. He
may be a romancer, a fictionist, an effect-seeker. Or he
may be the one who has his tongue in his cheek, as has
been suspected of some of the statements attributed to
Strauss; such as the musical depiction of red hair for
one of the divinities in his tone-poem, "Don Juan". If,
with Strauss, there has been reason for the critic to regard with wary eyes some of the detailed programmatic
disclosures credited to the composer, with Mahler, there
has been equal reason to suspect sundry instances of
"program" where the composer vehemently asserted
none existed. Whatever Berlioz said of his music in his
Memoirs has to be construed in the light of his colorful
descriptions of various incidents that never happened or
were in some material aspect different from his lively
accounts of them. The critic must forever sit as censor
on *indirect data*. But he cannot ignore it. It may lead
him astray. As often, it will prevent him from being led
astray. In the end it will be found to safeguard him,
also, against his tendency to harden his views into those
of musical pedantry. It will help him to preserve the essential relation of music to humanity. It will be his con-
stant reminder that music was written by men, for men,
and, unless we are to concede to it a divinity that separates it utterly from all other arts, about men. It will

save him from the notes that are only the symbols—it will save him from symbols, when it is the sound that matters—and it will save him from sound when mere virtuosity or sumptuosity in sonorities plays a tattoo on his nervous system, bowling him over one day with music that he will see as meretricious on the next.

BOOK THREE

APPRAISAL OF PERFORMANCES

APPRAISAL OF PERFORMANCES

Introduction

The greater part of the newspaper critic's labor is concerned with the quality and character of performances. Much as he might prefer to have his duties otherwise constituted, he soon discovers that his newspaper readers expect him to hold his mirror up to pianists, violinists, singers, string quartets, choruses and orchestras just as painstakingly and as analytically as to the music, new or old, that is at bottom his heart's concern. He may have moments when he resents the dominance of personality, at what seems to be the sacrifice of art. He may weary of the endless procession of executants, mostly mediocre or worse, upon whom all words seem wasted, in view of programs that are merely repetitions, one of another, and designed primarily to place the performer in the best possible light. He may feel that there is nothing contributive in the mere exhibition of how well a soprano can sing her high notes, or a pianist run octaves, or a violinist do double-stopping. But if he is the good journalist he ought to be, he will remember that simple reporting is an important part of his function; that each concert has its place in the news. Although the reporter describing a ship disaster, a political meeting or a stock market flurry can let the facts speak for themselves, the music critic has to call in opinion, in order to supply the facts. It has often been said, for instance, that correct pitch is a matter of fact and not of opinion. So it would be, if pitch were ascertained by some infallible mechanism. By no means is there always agreement between critic and layman, or critic and critic, as to whether a singer is above or below pitch, or squarely on the note. A review that made no mention of persistent flatting would scarcely have been a good job of reporting, for certainly this was one of the news facts of the particular recital.

As with pitch, so certain details that are more clearly matters of opinion—the quality of the voice, for instance, the freedom of its use—become virtually news facts which the reviewer cannot ignore. There are occasional brief notices of recitals, so perfunctory as to give only the name of the recitalist, the place and time of the recital, and some reference to the program. They usually have to do with events in which the public has shown a minimum of interest. Not only is such a review in no sense music criticism, but it would be very poor reporting if any considerable number of readers of that newspaper had a lively desire to know something about the recital in question.

The critic, then, approaches a recital or concert in the spirit of the reporter looking for facts. He finds most of his facts in the manner of the performance. He brings to bear all he has in technical knowledge, in accumulated experience, in ability to cleave to the essentials, in order that he may ascertain these facts. There are aesthetic considerations that may transcend facts. These and the critic's cultural background may play the larger part in shaping for him his answers to questions of interpretation and of the imaginative or poetic quality of a performance; answers that he may state in his review with the finality of facts. There could be endless hair-splitting as to where fact ends and opinion begins. This is all of small consequence, however, when we remember that it is as easy to disagree about a supposed fact like that of pitch, as about a "reading" which one critic says had spontaneity, another says had not; surely opinion rather than fact.

As has been emphasized, this is not a book of aesthetics. It is not even a book of any "higher criticism". Its ends are primarily pragmatic. It must abjure, therefore, all flights into the speculative with respect to what constitutes imagination, poetry, spontaneity, even personality, in the performance of music. These are the intangibles which each critic must sense for himself, in that "relation of two variables" which Lawrence Gilman has repeatedly dwelt upon, in discussing for the benefit of his readers the critical function. Let the prospective critic browse far and wide in the reading and the study that may quicken his perception of these intangibles. He will still need to know what he is looking for, in getting at the more mundane facts as to just how this recitalist is using his piano, voice, or violin, or how this string quartet, chorus or orchestra is meeting the requirements of the ensemble music it is undertaking.

The Piano Recital

Let us consider first the piano recital, stripped to those bare fundamentals which are to the critic substantially what the news facts are to a news reporter. The intangibles will scarcely be his first concern, though by the time he leaves the hall they may have outweighed everything pertaining to the recitalist's technical mastery of the resources of his instrument. Most commonly, the critic's first thought will be of tone. With the first chord or figuration he may look for the line at the end of the printed program which tells him what make of piano is being played. It is an unwritten law of the profession that the piano maker is never named in the review. Sometimes this law is not quite fair to the recitalist and unduly protects the piano. It may be reasoned, however, that if the recitalist uses an instrument that lessens the possibilities for power or for beautiful tone, the fault is solely his own. The critic may have his own opinions on what the advantages and the limitations of the various instruments are; and in the piano he may find an explanation for part, if not all that he may not like in a pianist's tone. But when he comes to write his review, he is concerned with the tone and not with the instrument.

There may be many secondary considerations with respect to the tone, other than a fundamentally musical

and singing quality. These will only become clear to him
as the recital progresses. Inevitably, they will involve
power and gradations of dynamics; since a beautiful,
feathery pianissimo sometimes consorts with blurr and
loss of musical quality when heroic resonance is desired.
Gradations of tonal quality as well as gradations of
dynamics will be noted, either in their presence or their
absence. Monotony of tone, even if it pertains to a richly
musical tone, will not escape his attention. His nose for
news will direct him to the issue of nuance—not merely
for its own sake, since its importance may very well be
chiefly in relation to questions of interpretation and
those intangibles he must sense as the recital develops.
But he is not interested professionally (however much
he may be interested personally, if he is himself a pianist) in *how* this tone is produced, how these gradations
of power and nuances of color are achieved. He is not
concerned with the performer's method. His eyes may
take due note of certain physical aspects of the performance, and he may even venture a reference to them for
descriptive purposes, but it is not his business to say that
the tone is good or bad *because* of a certain arm motion,
wrist position or angle of the fingers. To repeat once
more our tedious maxim, the critic is not a super-teacher.
These are the considerations of the pedagogue. The results, not the means, are what the mirror must reflect.

In conjunction with tone, the critic may be thinking,
with the first phrase, of the question of pedalling. His
primary concern is clarity. Beyond this fundamental
will be various details as to particular passages in par-

ticular compositions, carrying over into matters of conception and interpretation. There may be no reason to make any reference to pedalling. But if there is, the good reporter will recognize it as among the "facts" of the recital.

Dexterity of fingering and the clearness with which passages, easy or difficult, are played, are considerations that will keep his mind running at a gallop. Wrong notes and dropped notes may be of little consequence or they may be the badges of insufficient technique or slovenly performance. It is for the critic to decide which. He will scarcely be able to make that decision if he ignores them or simply does not know they are there. He may have other and larger issues to occupy him, both in his listening and his writing, to the eventual exclusion of petty slips; that is for the recital in question to decide; it is by no means a foregone conclusion.

Speed is one of the by-products of dexterity. Speed can be exciting, it can even be appropriate and enhance the artistry of a performance. But the critic will check speed against the need for speed, when he comes to deal with the intangibles and with interpretation. There are not many compositions in which it may be assumed that the composer wished them played, as Schumann has specified in one of his, as "fast as possible" and then "still faster". To report speed is to report a news fact; to declare it excessive is rightfully a prerogative of the critic and he may report it, according to his lights, with all the finality of fact. There are, of course, metronome markings that can be regarded as making fact rather than opinion of the time at which a composition or a passage should be played. But this, too, can lead to hair-splitting, since it can be contended with much force in various instances that metronome marks, particularly in older compositions, do not mean what they specify. On the face of things, rhythms also are facts. In practice, they are often as much a matter of opinion as is time; the critic, in fulfilling his function, often makes his opinion his fact.

Concerned, as he must be, with structure and proportion in the projection of any composition by a pianist, the critic will note not only the tracing of thematic contours, but the weight of one part as against another, whether in music of a polyphonic character, a melody treated harmonically, or a succession of chords and figurations. Here, too, he is concerned with the results, not with the reasons for the good or bad playing. He may refer to the very common fault of one hand slightly anticipating another, but this is description, not correction. He may prick up his ears over some bit of deft differentiation between the hands, but this for him is fact and not pedagogy. Octave passages, sixths and thirds, glissandi, innumerable details of passage work which may represent an achievement in themselves, are his concern, but in not the same way that they are the concern of a student. The critic must relate these things to the effect of the composition as a musical entity; to its structure, its meanings, its emotional communication, its style and its traditions, which are as much the issue as any purely pianistic detail. To do this, he cannot have too extensive a knowledge of piano literature. With it must go a perception of what compositions are primarily virtuoso show and what works use the resources of the instrument as the means and not the end.

The Violin

If virtuosity for its own sake is one of the problems of the piano recital, even less is it to be evaded when the recitalist is a violinist dealing with what, by and large, is a showier and more obvious type of music. The critic may even come to think first of a violinist in terms of his programs. It is taken for granted that a pianist can prepare any number of programs that will be musically worth while. The violinist has to scratch (sometimes in more ways than one) for material that is neither hackneyed, faded, flashy, popular or trivial, if he is to undertake several entirely different programs in the course of a season. But the violin, like the human voice, has a way of relating music to humanity and thus making treasurable to its listeners music that would not pass muster as music for the piano, the organ or the orchestra. Since it cannot always be on the peaks of a Bach or a Mozart sonata, the Beethoven or Brahms concerto, there is reason to rejoice that the violin has such brilliant possibilities in bravura and that it sings even the trivial so divinely well.

As a parallel to a primary consideration in dealing with the piano, the critic who sits in judgment on the qualities of a violin recital may think first of tone.

Its depth, richness and fullness, its purity and its vitality, or the lack of these attributes, will at once catch and hold the ear. But he will have an immediate concern that did not arise at the piano recital, that of the correctness of the intonation, often not merely the intonation of individual notes but of whole phrases that may be slightly sharp or flat. He will have questions of dexterity and speed to consider, as in his appraisal of a pianist, but with many details peculiar to the violin, as in double-stopping, spiccato, pizzicato, harmonics and under-use or abuse of vibrato; all of the many effects that resolve themselves into technique of the fingers and technique of the bow. Again, however, the results (not the method productive of these results) will determine what he writes. For the sake of description, he may make mention of a particularly high position of the bowing arm, or of the contrary in the instance of a recitalist who holds the elbow closer to his side, just as he may note, for the sake of the picture, the stridings, the rockings, and the hair-tossings of some spectacular fiddler; but it is not required of him that he shall say that the playing was any better or the worse because of these things. If he chooses to do so, he may; but he is entering another field vastly more specialized than that of criticism whenever he goes *behind* the facts in quest of the reason, and he invites challenges of a sort he can well do without, since merely to report the facts as he finds them is to confront contradiction at every turn.

In the sensuous appeal of its tone and in the emotional stir it can create by the simple singing of a melody, as well as by the excitement it can engender in virtuoso display, the violin may be said to exist for its own sake much more than the piano; with the result that much violin music has been written by violinists, primarily for the purpose of bringing out the special qualities of the instrument. Inevitably, the performer of this music is compelled to approach it in the virtuoso spirit; the question is not so much one of what this music is, as of what can he do with it. The critic will often have cause to consider the extent to which a violinist combats and defeats the temptation to make his mastery primarily a medium for display, and it is in this light that he may look indulgently upon a liberal use of transcriptions that otherwise were better left in their original form. There have been, and are today, noble musicians among violinists, whose programs are chosen with an eye primarily to musical worth. But it may be profitable to bear in mind a German critic's unfavorable summation of what he regarded as the basic fault of a group of famous violinists who were products of the same celebrated master: that they thought in terms of the wooden box held to the shoulder, and of the sounds that could be drawn from that box; rather than the printed page that was placed before them and what that page could be made to say. Like all such generalities, this one may not be quite just. But it can be construed as stating the case for a type of recital in which tone and technique carry the artist to a triumph the critic may feel was not a particularly high manifestation of the musical art. Technique for technique's sake we have with us, always.

The Singer

The critic who never names the make of the piano and rarely specifies whether the violinist plays a Stradivarius or a Guarnerius, has an immediate duty of diagnosis with regard to a singer's voice. She may have been booked as a contralto and her first phrases convince him that she is a soprano. He has to hold his mirror up to that voice. He must reflect its quality as he must reflect its compass and its power. A first question to be answered pertains to the kind of voice. This is not for the purpose of setting the singer on a different track or confirming her on the one she already has taken. It is to enable the reader to hear that voice as the reviewer heard it. There is the same concern with tone that occupies the critic in dealing with the piano and the violin, but it goes farther in that it involves a diagnosis of the organ producing the tone.

With considerations as to the richness, fullness, sweetness and responsiveness of the tone, will arise at once that of its steadiness. The vibrato that is cultivated on the violin and 'cello, and which, of course, is impossible on the piano, may be a glaring fault of an otherwise pleasurable production. Unsteadiness in any of its several forms—vibrato, tremolo, wobble, shake; fine distinctions that need not concern us here—will no more be ignored by the conscientious reviewer than a downright ugly quality of voice. On one occasion it may seem much less important, because of other attributes of the voice,

than on another when it serves to defeat whatever the
singer undertakes. The critic may note many things he
does not write, just as the news reporter accumulates an
excess of secondary facts and confines himself to the
essentials. Each recital, like each news happening, is
something unto itself. But the touchstones, as distinct
from what goes into the chronicle, remain about the
same for all.

Unsteadiness of tone usually brings up the question
of breath support. Of all the things the critic will flee,
as from the plague, is the question of a proper method
of breathing, one of the rocks on which the teaching
profession splinters itself into uncountable fragments.
The critic does not care a fig how a singer breathes, if
only she will have the breath to sustain her phrases after
she has made an attack that is clean and firm, and if she
will refrain from breathing so audibly or so visibly as to
cause the process to intrude upon the song. He may
take occasion to record that an artist's breathing was
effortless or was labored. To do so is merely to record
the fact and not to be concerned with the method. A
singer's breathing is of importance to the critic, not because it is "right" or "wrong" but because it either does
or does not make for a good legato, for mastery of the
long phrase, for ability to spin out soft notes when the
music calls for this, for the purity of the sound and the
firmness of the attack, and for the continued steadiness
of the tone. Tremolo and windiness are just as bad, be
the method the one that the old masters taught in the
times of the Porpora or the newest revolutionary dis-

covery of the vocal scientist who can prove that it is the spinal column and not the diaphragm that controls the stream of air.

The perfect scale, graduated as to weight and quality from top to bottom, is such a rarity that the critic has no expectation of having to write about it very many times in the course of a decade. But it is his mental measuring stick for every vocal recitalist when he comes to deal with this important, but not necessarily decisive item of equipment. If it is obvious that "registers" should not be, it is equally obvious that they are. So, too, the holes that commonly are to be found in the fringes of these "registers" and are bridged over adroitly or clumsily, in many and various ways. The critic takes note of them, though he may not always feel that it is necessary to speak of them. He does not consider that it is incumbent on him to devote a line, a paragraph or half a column to telling the singer why these holes are there and how she can go about eliminating them. There are singing teachers for that purpose. Newspapers doubtless have their own reasons for not employing these teachers to write the reviews.

Freedom of production is sometimes to be determined by the eye as well as the ear, but more often it is to be sensed only in the quality of the tone. In that quality may be discoverable a sense of strain or constriction when the artist is neither turning purple in the face, contorting her brow, stiffening her jaw, lifting her shoulders or clenching her hands. The critic may have very positive views on what it is that causes a "throaty" or a "pinched" tone, and he may use those descriptive terms for what they are worth in passing on the sound of that tone to his readers; but if he wishes to be a singing teacher he should hang up his shingle with the others rather than devote the space of his newspaper to highly debatable questions of voice placement, open or covered tones, carrying the medium up or the head down; except as these observations may justify themselves in being *descriptive* (for the reader) rather than *corrective* (for the artist). To comment on a beautiful, floating pianissimo as "pure head tone" is one thing. To rebuke an artist who produces a beautiful tone at the top of his compass because it apparently is not a head tone is quite another. There may be reason to believe that the shores of the vocal seas are strewn with wrecks of those whose methods were disastrous, but a beautiful sound remains a beautiful sound, however it is produced, a fact more germane to today's criticism than the possible loss of a beautiful organ five or ten years hence. The critic has the right to prophesy. He may even feel it his duty to prophesy, either because a very beautiful voice is at stake or because there is danger of false emulation on the part of worshipful students. But this is one of those extensions of the critical function previously referred to, in which the critic chooses to be something more than a critic in the belief that he is rendering a public service.

Phrasing, which is a matter of conscious art—circumscribed, it is true, by the physical matter of breath control—is even more the concern of the critic in the song recital than in the piano or violin recital, because it in-

volves word sequences and textual meanings as well as
the curve and import of the musical line. With diction,
phrasing will have an importance to the critic not only
for its own sake, but in enabling him to form an appraisal of the singer's sense of style.

Some elements of style must be sought among the
intangibles, but the presence or absence of legato, the
use and abuse of portamento, the relation of degrees of
power to the nature of the musical and the verbal phrase,
the degree of tranquillity or of explosiveness in the attacks, and the manner of intensifying emotional effects,
whether by tonal coloring or some violent effect such as
the operatic sob, will resolve themselves into readily applicable criteria. The singer who alternates loud and
soft notes for their own sake, or for the sake of contrast
only, will be recognized as one of little more artistry
than the singer who sings loudly all the time. Pianissimo
tones can be as cheaply sensational as ear-splitting loud
tones, if they are interjected purely as effect, without
any real reason existing therefor in either text or music.
So, too, the soft note that is an octave leap at the close
of a song in place of the note that is written there. This
book cannot attempt to show wherein the Mozart style
differs from the Hugo Wolf style, or the Bach style
from the Brahms style. It must be assumed that with
these, as with purely musical considerations of an adequate background, the prospective critic already has
passed the need of any such enlightenment. Needless
to say, he will have occasion to point out distinctions of
style many times in his reviews.

Every now and again some one with a laudable respect for the correctness of words will venture to point out that English dictionaries do not authorize the use of the term "diction" as an equivalent for pronunciation, enunciation or any aspect of vocal delivery. Webster, for instance, would limit it to the diction of a writer, in the sense of word-succession and sentence structure. But this is merely one of many instances of a word that has come into the language twice, the second time with a particular meaning. Diction, in the singer's or speaker's parlance, is a word adopted from the French. No doubt, vocal teachers were using it in the specific sense that has now become almost universal, long before it began to trouble word purists. It is a necessary word and doubtless is with us for good; going further, as it does, than enunciation or pronunciation and including them both, along with subtler considerations of the refinement, the grace, the poise and the charm of word projection. Diction may be clear and yet not of the aristocracy that is required for song; or in attaining that aristocracy it may have lost vigor and become precious in a degree that falsifies a song. All such questions apply with equal force to as many languages as the recitalist may venture to sing.

Mannerisms concern the critic if they cheapen or otherwise mar the effect of the singing. Theatricality usually does so in the recital hall. Gestures are commonly out of place. At the other extreme is the gawky or abashed singer who is sadly in need of stage presence. There are singers who seem to direct the voice to the inner ear and lack the sense of "putting it over". The critical mirror will reflect these things, according to their importance to the total achievement. Imagination, penetration to the heart of the verbal and musical substance, the ability to communicate a poetic or dramatic mood, the little touches of humor or sympathy by which a song is in some way related to life, these are intangibles that must be sensed. Often they are inextricably bound up with questions of style; yet it is conceivable that an artist might sing an exacting Mozart aria with impeccable style and project nothing of its poetic glow. The achievement of a mood is as often a matter of a personal identification with the song as it is of any conscious art on the part of the recitalist. For the reviewer, the mood either was or was not achieved. Why, is not his concern.

The critic has to learn that studio perfection, or approach to perfection, however laudable it may be, is not the open sesame to vocal success. The perfect scale, the faultless breath support and control, the elegant diction and the mastery of style that the conscientious pedagogue labors to bring about, may as often be found approximated by nonentities as by the reigning favorites. Whether this was always so is an issue of historical dispute. The truth that must be faced with regard to singers of today is that it is not the model vocalist (if such there be) but the singer of some unusual or remarkable attribute to distinguish her from the generality who wins and holds the public ear. This attribute may be found in the quality of the voice, in its volume, its compass, or some aspect of its compass, or in the artist's personality or emotional power; whatever it is that is highly individual to that artist and enables her to bring to her listeners something distinctive and stimulating because it is rare.

The nearly perfect vocalist, being an even greater rarity, might command equal success. It is not so much the business of the critic to lament this rarity as it is for him to be able to put his finger on the secret of each artist who does succeed. His review should show what this singer has and has not, what she can do and what she cannot do. Thereby he may clarify many an image likely to be confused by a multitude of listeners who have been enchanted or fascinated, not by beautiful singing but by a voice, a personality, a theatrical gift or some freak extension of resonance or range.

The question of singers' programs will bear no end of study. But in dealing with them the critic should not forget that the song recital, like every other musical event, is concerned primarily with *music,* not with quirks of words and bits of character projection. These things have their place, particularly in the programs of the diseuse. But the song recital of scant musical value, however amusing and entertaining it may be, and no matter how admirably sung, must be mirrored for what it is. Too often this means some justification of the unconscious distinction drawn in those notices and signs still to be encountered at church socials and the like, announcing "music and singing". There is plenty of music in the repertory of song. The recitalist who prefers the sentimental ballad and the bit of foolery that draws a laugh has made his choice.

The Ensemble—Chamber Music

In all chamber music, whether it is that of the sonata recital, the trio, the string quartet or some larger ensemble, style and mutuality—the interdependence of the players—are predominant considerations for the critic. Unity of purpose, unity of understanding, unity in achievement, are essentials. But mutuality goes beyond unity. It involves a give and take, a plurality within unity, whereby there is a shifting in some measure of leadership from player to player in many compositions, not merely a continuous parity of interest and effort. Good individual playing is, of course, of critical concern, because of its bearing on the quality of the ensemble. But the many instances in which the individual playing is admirable when the ensemble is lacking in mutuality (often because of differences of style or the intrusion of personal mannerisms) soon set the critic on the track of this fundamental of elasticity in interplay, a sort of fluidity in teamwork, as the first issue he has to settle. Beyond that are many considerations of musicianship, of penetration of the spirit as well as of the style of the composition, of mood projection and taste, as essential to their bearing on the quality of a performance as cleanness, clarity, balance, vigor or delicacy, nuances of color or dynamics, and tonal beauty. Patrician playing is for the patrician ear. The mirror may have its most subtle reflections to make in dealing with music of this order.

The Choral Ensemble

As some choral music calls for performances not unlike those of instrumental chamber music—madrigal singing, for instance—whereas other choral music approaches the symphonic in what may be termed vocal orchestration, this is a form of music that will require many and varied adjustments of the critical perspective. Balance of parts and clarity, whether in harmonic masses or polyphonic voices, will ordinarily be a first thought. The quality of the voices, whether fresh and vital, or worn and dull, will soon be made manifest. The critic will note attacks and releases, phrase beginnings and phrase endings, the precision of entrances, the unity of final chords, for signs of raggedness and insufficient preparation. There will be questions about the prominence of "inner voices", as in orchestral performances. Matters of time and rhythm will occupy him no less than in solo performances, whatever their nature. Mood projection may be much more a matter of dynamics than it is in solo singing, since the more personal qualities of poetic suggestion will scarcely be involved in the collective tone, save as it reflects the conductor's interpretation. Diction will scarcely be an issue with large choral bodies, but purity of vowels and sharp accentuation of consonants may enhance the musical effect. Style is the business of the conductor and can be very important. The B Minor Mass of Bach in the spirit and manner of the Prologue to Boito's "Mefistofele" or the Rossini "Stabat Mater" would call for vigorous language. The Mozart, Cherubini, Berlioz, Brahms and Verdi Requiems inhabit just so many different worlds. A literature that can embrace a Palestrina Mass and a Handel Oratorio, the Elgar "Dream of Gerontius" and the Lambert "Rio Grande" will require no end of distinctions; but they are mostly broad ones, so that the reviewing of choral performances is about as standardized as anything the critic ordinarily has to confront; and because of this, sometimes leaves him with surprisingly little to say.

The Orchestra

In dealing with orchestral performances, the critic has two cardinal considerations, other than the merit and character of the music performed. The one is the quality of the ensemble, the degree of excellence of its playing; the other is the nature and quality of the "reading" or interpretation. In fewer words, one is the *orchestra,* the other the *conductor.* The importance of the conductor is a relatively recent development in orchestral music. In the Germany of Wagner's youth, symphony concerts were given even at the Leipsig Gewandhaus without a conductor, the players following the bow of the concertmaster. Only when there was vocal music was the conductor deemed indispensable, to the end that the soloist or chorus might have an accompaniment that would hang together. We know that earlier, the musician who sat at the harpsichord and played the figured bass (often the composer) was the nearest equivalent to the modern conductor. It may be doubted, however, whether the change by which the conductor has become a commanding figure has been a greater one than that in the character and quality of orchestras.

Berlioz has some amazing stories to tell in his Memoirs of compositions that could not be played, either because the instruments were too few or the players incapable of getting over the notes. The first volume of Ernest Newman's "Life of Richard Wagner" proves rather conclusively the inadequacy of the orchestras of the first half of the last century to do justice to the music of Beethoven and his successors. He cites many instances to show that if the "advanced" music of that day was not understood it was because the performances were so wretched the music was denied all opportunity to be understood. Compositions we now hear from organizations of a hundred or more were attempted with fifteen, twenty or at the most forty instruments. Some instrumental parts, as Berlioz found during his visit to Germany, could not be played at all and simply had to be omitted. Not only was individual technique lacking, but ensembles were hit-and-miss in the instruments they had available. Old men were retained who were a dead loss to the ensemble. Liszt, at Weimar, the envy of most of Germany's court musicians, had to produce "Lohengrin" at its world premiere with an orchestra of thirty-eight pieces. Today there is often a question whether our symphonic ensembles are not too large for some of the music they play; there is a growing tendency among conductors to reduce their ensembles in the performance of the music of Mozart, Haydn and those who went before, so as to restore the original balance between strings and woodwinds and approximate more clearly the original quality of tone.

Today, the orchestra is the most sumptuous instrument of sound the human brain and human experience have evolved. Its possibilities probably are far from exhausted, in spite of the explorations of Berlioz, Liszt, Wagner, Strauss, Debussy and the moderns. So inviting are its capacities for the achievement of versicolorous polyphony, as well as massed harmony, that recent years have brought a flood of transcriptions of Bach, some of which have raised the question whether these cumulative sonorities, beggaring the organ and the klavier for which this music was written, are not more Bacchanalian than Bachian. Orchestras have come to be judged by the richness, the fullness, the vitality, the opulence of color of their tone—whether mass tone, the group tone of the separate choirs, or the solo tone of individual chairs. Experience with many orchestras is of value in any such appraisal. To have heard the strings of the Vienna Philharmonic, for instance, is to be in a better position to judge the strings of the Boston Symphony. The tour of the New York Philharmonic abroad was something of a revelation in Germany, not as regards the strings but the woodwinds. The golden brass of Toscanini's ensemble has meant a new standard in the brass playing of

American orchestras. The sensuous warmth and depth of tone of the Philadelphia Orchestra under Leopold Stokowski, if not equally appropriate to all compositions, has made the tone of various other orchestras sound shallow and superficial. The critic can no more avoid an evaluation, or at least a description of the quality of the orchestral sound than he can that of the voice of a singer; particularly, as this quality is found to change materially with a change of leadership.

The precision, the unity, the clarity and the balance of the playing are commonly to be charged up to the conductor. Playing that is muddled, rough or slovenly, may, however, indicate an inferior "instrument" as well as mediocre leadership. Precision and unity involve collective musicianship as well as decisiveness on the part of the man in authority. For the conductor, clarity and balance may entail much more than the correct playing of the notes. The critic cannot evade the moot question of the emphasis given "inner voices", as one conductor lifts one such voice into prominence and another stresses a different voice; though there may be many occasions when he will not regard these details as particularly worth talking about. So with questions of tempi, both the fundamental tempi and those fluctuations by which elasticity and grace are sought, sometimes at the expense of structure. Rubato, to the end of time, may be regarded as something of a synonym for "debatable". The critic will have his convictions in many instances. In others, he may be reluctant to decide that one way of playing a phrase or a movement is utterly wrong and another utterly right. The better he knows his scores, as a conductor knows them, the more pronounced these convictions may be. But nothing could be more dangerous to criticism than for a critic to study the standard symphonic répertoire with one of the first-rank conductors and then brand as incorrect and indefensible the tempi of all other conductors when they did not agree with what he had been taught. Obviously, if he had studied with one of the others, he would be exacting a different set of tempi. Perhaps no critic would be so intolerant as one who had been a practicing conductor. The critic's catholicity of experience gives him a liberality of judgment in such matters that will serve him better than ironclad conceptions as to what is irrevocably wrong or right. In details of tempi the musician much more than the layman is in danger of not seeing the forest for the trees.

There persists a maxim that if the tempi are right, the performance will be right. But the critic who knows more about tempi than all the disagreeing conductors has to have a sublime belief in himself. The less cocksure but ordinarily courageous writer will say his say when he feels that the occasion demands it. He will not dodge the issue if he is convinced the pace is too fast or too slow or so irregular as to involve a loss of momentum. But he will hesitate to condemn an otherwise superior performance, and one which achieves a stirring or beautiful effect, because he has preferred, or believed in, another tempo for this or that section or even whole movements of a symphonic work. To be a super-conductor in these matters is like being a super-teacher for singers, violinists, pianists—what a man!

With questions of tempi put in their place, with issues of tone quality, clarity, balance, precision and other ensemble details falling into alignment, with individual stresses such as those given inner voices noted for what they are worth, the critic will have still to consider the poetic and expressive qualities of the performance, the intangibles that enter into the communication of emotion and mood. He may sense without difficulty that of two performances of the same symphony one is eloquent and one is dull; one is poetic and one is lacking in imagination; one is tremendously vital and one simply does not spark. He may not be able to put his finger on the reason for any of this, so far as the playing or the visible aspects of the conducting are concerned. He can only note it and report it as a fact. Should the conductor then ask him, "what do you mean when you say my performance lacked poetry?", he might be hard put to explain. But his mirror would not have reflected that concert if he had hesitated to deal with what, in the end, may have been its most important characteristic.

FOLLOWING THE SCORE

To assume that a critic invariably knows an orchestral score as a conductor knows it, that he carries piano sonatas in his head as a recitalist does, or that he has memorized the various markings which guide violinists or singers in the performance of programs which may embrace as many as twenty numbers, some in the manuscript, would be fantastic. Dotting i's and crossing t's is the pettiest sort of criticism and the most barren. The generality of the critic's readers will not be interested in details to the extent that another conductor is interested; or another pianist, another violinist or another singer who may happen to include the same numbers in his répertoire. Reviews are written for the many and not the few—except when, for particular reasons, they are written for the few and not the many.

It has been said several times in these pages that the critic is not a super-teacher. Scolding an artist about a misplaced accent, a detail of phrasing, an unnecessary aspirate in the turning of a vocal figuration, a fleeting moment of cloudy pedalling; or, with a conductor, an obscured inner voice or even an altered chord, is not worthwhile criticism, except as it may actually influence, appreciably and tangibly, the quality of the performance, either as to taste, style, balance, clarity, euphony or conviction. The artist who sins frequently or habitually in any direction may properly be called to book for faults that would be too inconsequential to mention if they were rare or only occasional. But it cannot be too tenaciously remembered that, ordinarily, criticism of a performance should concern itself with *that performance* and not with an artist's entire standing or position as established for the critic by *other* performances. No performance is any less faulty because its predecessors were much better. With even more emphasis, it must be said that a good performance is a good performance whatever the insufficiencies and the limitations the artist may have disclosed in other music. Every concert, every item of that concert, like each separate assumption of an operatic role, ought to be adjudged on its own merits and not in the light of something else.

These considerations bring us to the questions that arise with respect to the advisability of a critic "following with the score" at concerts, particularly concerts of orchestral music. There are arguments to be considered, for and against. It has been confessed that critics, unless they happen to be performers also, do not habitually "carry scores in their heads". They may be vague as to many details of the standard symphonies they know best. The conductor does something that puckers their brows. This is not the way a particular passage has sounded to them in other performances. Is he right and were the others wrong? If the critic had been following the score

he would have had his answer then and there. He may
have opportunity subsequently to consult a score, before writing his review. But he may forget, or be too
pressed for time. He may trust "tradition" and run a
certain risk in finding fault. Or he may "let it slide" and
ignore what otherwise might have been a point of particularized interest in his review. Without a score, conductor's cuts or other alterations may escape his knowledge, though he may have an indefinite feeling that all is
not as it should be. On the morrow he may learn, to his
own discomfort, of the righteous indignation of a con-
frere who, with the printed page before him, caught the
gentleman on the podium in the act of doing unconscion-
able things to the music of a master not to be improved
upon by his inferiors.

With other ramifications, these are the practical considerations in favor of following a performance with, or
from, the score. The reviewer then knows, or should
know, exactly what he is talking about. The notes will
bear him out.

But only too often these are not the issues he is going
to talk about. He may even be led into futile and tedious
discussion of details eminently not worth talking about.
The eyes have it. The ears play their part in a subor-
dinate capacity to the optics, noting chords, rests, sus-
pensions, tempo indications, instrumental doublings,
subsidiary figurations and the thousand and one considerations of structure, harmonic device and orchestration.
Larger issues, and particularly those which are qualita-
tive rather than provably factual, such as the poetry, the

imagination, the vitality, the personality or the distinction of a performance, may be lost in minor distractions and irritations that would have had no part in the listener's reactions if he had not been fettered by the notes. The letter and the spirit are still very different things in all that pertains to interpretation, much as the critic may believe that adherence to the letter is the first step in a conscientious fulfillment of the spirit. To be deeply engrossed with the letter may be to take more away from a free and just consideration of the spirit than the score-reader realizes in the concentration of the moment. He may magnify the importance of secondary details, even to the point of not seeing the forest for the trees. He may unwittingly divert his listening and his reviewing into the pettifogging business of dotting the i's and crossing the t's. He may find himself gravitating into the untenable role of super-teacher; this time the schoolmaster of conductors, correcting their performances as a pedagogue corrects papers or an editor corrects proof. This may be of value to him, in adding to his store of knowledge—it may even be good for the conductor to have brought home to him the knowledge that some one is checking up on his lesser peccadillos as well as on his more obvious sins of commission or omission—but it may also be fatal to the review.

There can be no rule, no very positive advice on this subject of score-reading. One individual will benefit more than another, one lose more than another. The coordination of eye and ear will be one thing for A, quite another for B. So, too, the question of the dominance of one faculty over the other. The critic can be both a score-reader and a non-score-reader, according to the particular circumstances. He may have special reasons to be on his guard, to want the corroboration of the notes, to play for the moment the role of score detective. Or he may, above all things, wish to win free of paper-music and hear things as they sound, not as they look; forgetting, for instance, a jugglery of key signatures and rhythmic changes which the eye perceives clearly enough but which dissipate themselves completely in a performance because of a multitude of things that simply do not "sound".

Obviously, the critic cannot know any score too well, except that to know much mediocre music intimately has involved an irremediable waste of time. Listening with a score is a sure prop to knowledge. If that knowledge can be acquired *before* the event, rather than *during* it, so much the better. Compromise is the eternal order of things and critics *do* contrive to go on educating themselves while endeavoring to pass on to their readers the benefits of prior preparation. But the mirror function takes precedence over self-improvement. The review itself is the task of the moment.

OPERA

He who scorns the theatre is not likely to be a sound critic of opera. The devotee of pure music, for whom even the program-symphony or tone-poem is obnoxious because it harnesses music to some literary or other extra-musical chariot, almost certainly will lack the sympathy necessary to grasp and properly evaluate the relation of the music to the dramatic action which is a fundamental in all criticism of opera. The critic need not believe that opera or music-drama is the highest form of music to acknowledge that it is one of the most potent and expressive forms of art. Every opera is in some degree that synthesis of which Wagner and others have postulated, and the approach to it, whether that of the composer, the listener or the critic, is the synthetical one. A beautifully sung but badly acted performance may bring ridicule from the least informed member of the audience. A work well sung and adequately acted, but wretchedly staged, may be disappointing, because it is disillusioning, for the person who is fastidious about music. In spite of its absurdities, as proclaimed from the housetops for at least two centuries, opera holds its place primarily because of illusion; the same music with-

out the stage trappings and action rarely exerts anything like the same power in this respect, except (as in
the case of the Wagner excerpts played on symphonic
programs) when the listeners build for themselves a
mental stage that is mostly glorified memory of what
they actually have seen, or read about.

The critic, then, needs to think of opera in terms of
the theatre, not of the concert hall. If he finds operatic
acting different from the acting of the spoken stage,
this, for the most part, is because operatic acting is inferior. Occasionally a Chaliapin proves that there is no
fundamental reason for a radically different technique,
except that words are sung on varying pitches and in
time, instead of being spoken freely. The tendency to
excessive gesturing on the operatic stage has been de-
fended on the basis that operatic acting must be more
pictorial than acting in drama. Antonio Scotti, one of
the most convincing of latter-day operatic actors, was
ever a singer of few gestures. The tendency to posturize
roles may be regarded as an evidence of how closely related opera is to ballet in the minds of many of its tech-
nicians.

The critic will have his own opinions on what constitutes good operatic acting. He will need them. He cannot shut his eyes to the stage and fancy he is hearing a
string quartet or a symphony. So, too, with the settings,
the costumes and all that pertain to *mis-en-scène*. He
has need for much the same historical sense and knowledge of various periods that the dramatic critic requires.
His background should tell him what is an anachronism

and what is permissible or stimulating in the way of stylization. He may know he protests vainly, yet continue to protest against sheer silk stockings for peasant girls, high-heeled slippers instead of medieval shoon, creations that are gowns and not costumes. His mirror has all these things to reflect and it can no more pass over a ridiculous botching of the fight in the last act of "Tristan und Isolde" than it can pass over bad singing of the "Liebestod". In no other branch of his critical work, will the extent of his background mean so much. The critic who knows little but music will be at no end of disadvantage in dealing with opera, able as he may be in his appraisal of vocal technique and orchestral playing, and in musical analysis.

Varying types of opera are not to be appraised in terms of each other. Mozart's "Marriage of Figaro" is none the less a masterpiece because it blithely disputes most of the principles governing the Wagner "Ring des Niebelungen". "Wozzeck" is not to be condemned off-hand because it is antithetical to "Aïda". "Pelléas et Mélisande" will never stand or fall on its likeness or unlikeness to "Norma" or "Der Freischütz". "Boris Godounoff" has greatness that proves nothing whatever in estimating "Cenerentola" or "Rosenkavalier". "Rigoletto" and "Traviata" are masterpieces, irrespective of "Elektra" and "Salomé". "Don Giovanni" and "Fidelio" will not be appraised in terms of "Götterdämmerung". The experienced critic knows there are good works and bad works of every type. He must have the catholicity, the universality of taste to deal intelligently and fairly with a multitude of types, representing a diversity not only of means but of ends. A good aria remains a good aria, a good sextet a good sextet, however strongly he may incline toward the type of music-drama that does away with arias, sextets and all set numbers. The critic will not scorn "Die Meistersinger" because of the Prize Song or the Quintet, or "Die Walküre" because of Wotan's Farewell. He may even find ground for legitimate criticism of Verdi's masterly "Falstaff" because of the manner in which airs that seem to be trembling on the lips of the principals (as with Fenton in the final scene) are ruthlessly shut off—as if the octogenarian composer had said, "Go to! I will show you that I, too, can write opera without tunes".

The critic will have need to be conscious of—indeed, he will have scant opportunity ever to forget—the thread that has run through opera from the first, and has been the starting point of each of the several historic reforms, by which music has been pledged and repledged to service in behalf of the word—the handmaiden of drama. As every conservatory student should know, the Florentines, in the belief that they were restoring the principle of the Greek drama, regarded opera as a form of sung speech, and from that day to this, through three centuries and more, the lyric drama has swung like a pendulum away from and back to its original conception.

Music is a jealous jade. Either she rules or she sulks. That is why there is so little "incidental" music, so-called, that is important as music. The secondary role is

not for her. The Florentines, bent on giving emotional
expressiveness to the word, wrote music that is beautiful in its own right. Monteverdi went further; music
became the dominant power in his alliance of the arts.
Eventually it so monopolized interest that opera was
more concert than opera. Gluck preached a return to
the hegemony of the word; but like the Florentines he
wrote beautiful music. The melodious Italians again
waged war on the old ideal. Opera swung back to a tune
basis, with music, not drama, the goal. Wagner repeated
in his different way the Gluck revolution. Again, however, what he passed on to posterity was a glory of music. In our own day, we have had "Pelléas" and "Wozzeck" to represent the Florentine conception of music
for drama's sake. But we have discovered that in "Pelléas", Debussy—like the Florentines, like Gluck, like
Wagner—is living on *for music's sake*. We are not yet
certain about "Wozzeck". But if there is any one lesson
to be drawn from this apparent conflict between opera
written for music's sake and opera written for drama's
sake, it is that the latter often produces the better
music. It is when music is pandered to that she turns
courtesan. Tune for tune's sake invites cheapness and
triviality. Like the Florentines, Gluck, Wagner and
Debussy hitched the musical wagon to a star of ideality.
Instead of entering service as handmaiden to drama,
their music became a transfiguring and a redemptive
force which transcended their drama. Because of the
increased importance of the orchestra in Wagnerian and
post-Wagnerian music-drama, excerpts from works

of this genre have had an importance to the concert repertory beyond anything which could feasibly be ex-
tracted from the song-operas. This, certainly, has been
a triumph for music as music, not music-drama. These
excerpts have not become absolute music, however, by
reason of this transference from the stage to the concert
hall. The purist cannot claim them. Whatever his preference, the critic must recognize that much of the finest
and most exalted inspiration that has gone into music of
any order was poured into the receptacles of opera. He
must meet it on its own terms or he is likely to be of
little service to his newspaper and to his readers, or to
this particular manifestation of a many-sided art.

Of operatic music, the critic may ask many questions:
Is the melodic stuff good, bad or indifferent? Is the music vocal; does it sing well? Is it cunningly contrived, so
that it moves always forward, or is it a series of halts and
new beginnings? Does the music itself, even though the
opera be one of set numbers, carry forward the action
or do the airs and concerted pieces serve as impediments?
Is the score well orchestrated, for its period, with a
measure of resourcefulness and originality, even if it
functions chiefly as a big guitar? Is there characteriza-
tion in this music, or do all the personages sing much
the same cast of melody? Does the orchestra characterize
and make itself an integral part of the drama, or is it
something apart, a decorative accompaniment or a com-
petitive symphony? Is there a suggestion of time and
place in the music or does it ring a little false as to the
period, the locale and the stage personages? Does it con-

vey the emotions of the operatic characters? Does it
intensify the situations of the drama? In the end, has it
built illusion, either by means of its own appeal as music
or by virtue of the manner in which it has heightened the
effect of other elements in the synthesis? Beautiful singing for its own sake, as in many of the older operas, and
sumptuous orchestral playing of a symphonic order have
their place in establishing mood and creating illusion.
The methods of Bellini are not those of Strauss.
"Norma" has as much of illusion, many will contend, as
has "Salomé".

Of the performance, the critic may ask: Is it well
sung? Is it expressively sung? Are the singers capable
of creating illusion in their physical appearance and in
the dramatic projection of their roles? Is there a competent ensemble or is each artist concerned only with
the effect of his part? Are the singers adequately heard
or is the orchestra usurping their prerogatives contrary
to the plain intention of the composer? Is the orchestral
score well played, whether thin or complex, a mere accompaniment or a symphonic fabric? Does the stage
direction carry conviction or is it a species of makeshift
and drab routine? Is the work well mounted or does it
have to succeed in spite of the scenery? Are the costumes
and other details correct or appropriate; or, if the work
has been stylized, has taste kept pace with imagination?
If there is a spectacle on a large scale, does the spectacle
contribute to, or detract from, the impact of the music
and the drama? Again, has it been a performance potent in illusion—illusion arising from beautiful singing,

vital acting, sumptuous orchestral playing, the magnificence of the spectacle, or the presence of several or all of these factors; no one of which can be considered unimportant to the success of the opera.

Appraisal of the dance, though it often gravitates to the music critics because newspapers seldom feel justified in having other special writers solely for this duty, involves quite another art and does not come within the scope of this discussion. Operatic ballets are not likely to get the music critic into deep water, but if his duties require him to deal with interpretative dancing he may find it expedient to make special preparation for his task. Significant music has been written for the mimetic drama. Some of it can be better appraised in the concert room than in the theatre, though it may gain in significance for the concert listener if he is able to summon forth the recollection of a stage performance. Ordinarily, the tendency is for the eye to over-ride the ear when minds visualize a musical scenario. Motion and spectacle have the first call.

THE COMPOSITE IDEAL

With long service and varied experience, particularly in dealing with opera, the music critic finds himself confronted by a situation in which to be true to his lights he must ask the improbable. He applies standards he knows are sound, yet which so transcend what he has any real prospect of encountering as to seem to justify the layman's description of him as hypercritical. Nothing that he asks is outside the realm of his own experiences. The ideal he seeks to apply is not a figment of the brain, remote from the art and technique of fallible human interpreters. He has seen, heard, felt it all. But never at one time or in one place. There is the rub. His is a composite ideal. One detail here. Another there. A third, ten years removed. A fourth in another country, half way around the globe.

The reviewer is called upon to consider a performance of Wagner's "Tristan und Isolde." He is not satisfied with the Tristan of the day, though this Tristan may be less wooden in action and vocally less given to self-strangulation than many another. In their own identities, the Tristans of the past may not trouble the reviewer at all. But he cannot be completely unconscious of the ghosts waiting to be summoned forth upon the stage of his memory. He knows that one man sang the music as he feels it should be sung. Why does not the Tristan now before him sing it that way? It has been done, therefore it can be done. Another's acting was superb. Why should this creature on the stage go through the old windmill motions again? There was none of that in the impersonation of the artist with whom, perhaps unconsciously, the present Tristan is being compared. The walk, the figure of still another Tristan, heroic to look upon, though of inadequate voice and of little resourcefulness as an actor, bring still another consideration to the mind. And how well an otherwise unimportant Tristan once costumed the part! In comparison, there is something drab about the figure on the stage, some want of distinction that is due to his clothes.

Here is nothing fantastic, nothing extreme. The critic is only applying the measuring rod of his own experience. But he has rolled a half dozen Tristans into one, taking from each the distinctive attributes, casting aside those that were commonplace. He asks of the man on the stage that he approximate all these, but only as to what was best in them. There is nothing surprising that he should find fault with the singing, when his own experience tells him how the work can and should be sung. He has every reason to be disappointed by acting that falls definitely short of the conviction he has known it to possess. He has seen Tristans who were heroic, who created illusion, so it is no marvel if he finds fault with the unimpressive figure before his eyes. It may be that he makes no conscious comparisons with any particular artist, but invokes a pre-conception of his own that a score of artists helped him to form. He has set a standard for the role no Tristan of his experience could have met in all of its exactions, although he arrived at that standard through them.

If this is true of one character, what happens to the performance as a whole when the composite ideal is applied all down the line, to Isolde, to Brangäne, to King Marke, to Kurwenal, to the conductor, to the stage management, to the inter-relations of the ensemble, to the lighting and the illusive element called atmosphere?

The standard of orchestral playing may have been largely determined by performances in which the casts were not particularly notable. The stage direction may have been the best when the orchestra was the worst. Exceptionally good lighting may have distinguished a representation with commonplace scenery. As every meritorious detail has tended to establish for the critic an objective that should be reached, or approximated, so the flaws and insufficiencies discoverable in the same performances have fortified him in his convictions as to what palpably is wrong and unacceptable. It has taken many performances to prove that he is right. But the fact remains that he *is* right. The flaws *are* flaws. Either he must enumerate them, or, assuming the attitude of one resigned to disappointments where performances of "Tristan" are concerned, omit from his review what he may justly regard as its essentials. For him, it was not a good performance. Many of his readers may have found it a thrilling one. If, in his dissatisfaction, he seems to tear everything to pieces, there may be nothing whatever of the hypercritical involved. He merely has had a truer grasp of what the work can be, and should be, in the theatre. Wagner at times lost interest in the production of his works because he gave up hope of finding satisfactory singers. He saw always the ideal, saw it undefiled and saw it whole. The most exacting critics may fall considerably short of the composer in this respect. But the critic's composite ideal is so much nearer the composer's than is ever likely to be realized for him in any given performance, that there are times when the work he wishes least to hear—knowing what to expect—is the one of which he is most passionately fond. In the words of Pitts Sanborn,* the man who boasted that he never missed a performance of "Meister-singer" could not have loved "Meistersinger" very well!

---

* Pitts Sanborn, music critic of the *New York World-Telegram.*

A DISCUSSION OF BANALITY.

Of all the intangibles with which the critic has to deal, none is more elusive or more omnipresent than the issue of banality. In his attempt to evaluate the basic material of any work, a first decision may very well have to be: Is it banal? All that the critic is in refinement of taste and breadth of nature, all that he possesses in intuition and penetration, all that he has acquired of knowledge and background, all he has accumulated of experience with every type and period of composition, enters into the answer to that question. The more he has heard, the more likely the answer is to be in the affirmative, since banality most often resolves itself into the trite, the overworked, the too-familiar. The "popular" is not necessarily the banal, since fresh and spontaneous ideas may be encountered in dance tunes, the while rubber-stamp platitudes exist in ponderous symphonies; but the sort of excessive popularity that causes a musical comedy "hit" to become the rage of two continents and leads to all manner of quick imitation, almost inevitably exhausts the vitality of the tune, with the result that banality claims it for its own. This early demise is not always a fair test of the worth of an idea. Many another melody accepted by the cognoscenti might have been killed off in the same way if it had ever been similarly popular. Its failure to make so general an appeal may have been due to some lack of spontaneity, rather than to any superior qualities. There is sometimes occasion for surprise on re-hearing, after a lapse of years, some popular tune that was done to death in its day, at the quality and the individuality of the virtually defunct melody.

This recognized, there is still the tendency to look upon that which savors of the "popular" as being banal. Undoubtedly, one of the touchstones to banality is here. The really fresh and spontaneous idea in popular music is not sufficiently common to offset the sweatshop product. Music ground out according to the pattern of the moment usually is full of borrowed phrases which repeat one another, *ad nauseam,* and which have associations and connotations from the lower levels of life. Aristocratic art may be sterile, but to be truly aristocratic it must be the opposite of banal. Therefore the patrician turn of phrase, not always as vital as something with an unmistakably "popular" stamp, is apt to fare better in criticism than is sometimes its due. The folk-song, incorporated in an art work, or transformed for symphonic purposes, may retain its essentially popular character and be a much more potent theme than many a tortuous product of meticulous refinement. But that folk-song is not necessarily banal because it is popular. It is banal if it is trite or cheap. The touchstone of aristocracy, therefore, is one limited in its applications.

The writer knows of no really dependable criteria for banality in music. Grove ventures no definition of the term. Webster takes no specific heed of the tonal art in the generalization: "Something commonplace, hackneyed or trivial; the commonplace in speech; trivialness." Applied to music, this is a matter for the individual ear and for that inevitable consensus of ears which must reckon on minority reports. In nothing more than in this issue of banality is beauty or worth in music that "relation between two variables", the work and the listener.

But there is another kind of banality in which the reason would seem to play a stronger part—reason at the service of taste. Banality may involve fitness; the issue of the appropriateness of the music to express or to carry out the program assigned to it. As has been emphasized before, the author has no desire to influence the musical opinions of any one who reads these pages; if critical judgments enter into this discussion, it is for the purpose of illustration or explanation of some point or procedure; the reader is not to assume that he is being asked to accept these opinions as of any value to him for their own sake.

In taking banality as our test, let our illustrations be two operas of widely divergent types, Richard Strauss's "Elektra" and Bedrich Smetana's "Bartered Bride". They inhabit different worlds. It may be argued that the two works cannot be compared. Technically they have little in common. Dramatically, they seek different ends. One is music-drama. The other, in the best sense of the term, is comic-opera. Granting all this, there would be nothing unreasonable about an application of the touchstones of banality to both, resulting in some critical declaration that, of the two, "Bartered Bride" is the more spontaneous and treasurable in melodic inspiration, whereas "Elektra" raises more seriously the issue of banality.

Comic-opera can have inspiration, music-drama can be banal. Wagner's "Die Meistersinger" is comic-opera at the same time that it is music-drama. The same theatre can house Mozart's divine "Così fan Tutte" and Schreker's dreadful "Singende Teufel". The circumstance that the first is comic-opera and the second music-drama will scarcely befuddle the issue as to where inspiration is to be found and where banality; all questions of period, style, weight, technique aside. In the great scene between Hans Sachs and Walther in the workshop of the cobbler, Wagner filled page on page of his "Meistersinger" score with thematic substance strikingly like that which supplies the nub of the Overture to Nicolai's "Merry Wives of Windsor". The fact that the latter is comic-opera, pure and simple, does not invalidate the theme, either for Nicolai or for "Meistersinger". But it would not do for "Parsifal" or "Tristan."

The Strauss "Elektra" remains a remarkable and even a thrilling work. But this is in spite of, rather than because of, its larger melodic expansions. Our contention is that such melodies as the opening chorus of Smetana's "Bartered Bride", the lilting Bohemian dances, the tender and sportive duets of Hans and Marie, Hans and Kezal and Marie and Wenzel, beggar in the quality of their inspiration the more songful moments that Strauss has permitted Elektra and Chrysothemis, and more particularly those cantilena passages for orchestra, glowing in sound though they are, which are developed in conjunction with Elektra's monologue and the Elektra-Orestes recognition scene. This has nothing to do with the technical virtuosity in which the Straussian material is clothed. There *is* involved, however, the question of *dramatic fitness,* along with that of the basic worth of the themes *per se.*

The passing of years has increased rather than diminished the popularity of Strauss. But it has resulted in something like unanimity of critical opinion as to his employment of banal themes in an indiscriminate manner disturbing to the fastidious, whatever the splendors of his orchestra or the complexity of his structure. In this respect, "Elektra" only repeats what is in the tone-poems. "Heldenleben" and "Death and Transfiguration" are none the less notable works because they contain themes we need not hesitate to call banal. Some of them smack of Munich beer halls. Others may remind us of fiddlers in knee-length leather pants encountered in the Bavarian uplands.

But is the tune from the Czech countryside any better, just because it is Czech? Is the Russian popular song superior to that of Naples, merely because it is Russian? Is a folk-tune from Finland superior to one from Sicily? Or are we likely to be misled into praising one because its idiom is relatively unfamiliar, the while we reject the other as banal because it has been in the musical larder of our particular section of the globe ever since we began to have a conscious musical art? There is the possibility that a rhythmic or melodic pattern, commonplace enough in its habitat, but tardy in getting abroad, may escape at the outset the tag of banality that would have been fastened on it if it had been the everyday story elsewhere that it was at home.

Returning to our "Elektra"-"Bartered Bride" comparison, we find opportunity to consider our second phase of banality, that which is not altogether a question of naked notes for their own sake; but of their *fitness* for the uses to which they are put. "Bartered Bride" is a peasant comedy. The peasant tunes belong. "Elektra", whatever the departures of the libretto of Von Hofmannsthal from the dramas of Sophocles, Euripides and Aeschylus, is not a reverie of the Pschorrbräu. The Munich brand of sentimental melody does not belong. There can be banality or lack of it in just this. The sort of melody that can assert charm in a song like "Traum durch die Dämmerung" can sound commonplace in an exalted drama of the ancients. This is partly because it suggests an utterly different sphere, a different locale and essentially different personages. Yet that melody might be altogether acceptable in "Rosenkavalier."

Among the champions of the music of our own times, there can be hot argument as to whether the Johann Strauss waltzes, so beloved by those who cling to the glamor of other days, are any less banal than the Gershwin type of jazz, since both are "popular" music, though of differing era, place and spirit. But put either in the second act of "Tristan" or the Grail scene of "Parsifal" and who would dispute their banality there! "The Bartered Bride" is of a piece. Its music fits. It rings true to time, place, people. If it sought to be Straussian or Wagnerian or Brahmsian, or even Humperdinckian, that music might be both inept and banal.

To recapitulate, banality in music involves these several criteria, no one of which is universal or final:

Is this music trite or fresh; rubber-stamp or individual?

Is it of the streets, possibly the gutter, or has it a patrician cast?

Is it apt and appropriate for its purposes, or is it, by reason of some alien suggestion or cheapening association, recognizably out-of-place?

The critic will have cause to remember that in varying measure banality is to be discerned in the harmonic substance and orchestral dress of a composition as well as in its melodic content. The criteria are much the same.

BOOK FOUR

THE WRITING

PREPARING COPY—PRACTICAL
JOURNALISM

Read

No good reason exists for any special concession to the music critic in the matter of the preparation of his copy. The newspaper that employs him to write about music expects of him the same adherence to fundamentals of newspaper practice that it expects of the men who write about sports, politics or the stock market. All are specialists. All are newspapermen. Ordinarily the specialist needs less surveillance, less check and double-check, less help from the copy desk than the news reporter. The specialist is assumed to have served his apprenticeship long since, to know the inner workings of the newspaper plant, to be dependable as to names and facts; and to have perfected the more mechanical aspects of his writing so that his language, his spelling, his sentence structure, his punctuation can go direct to the linotypes in the composing room without further verification, dictionary consultation and interlineation. Good or bad, the specialist's style usually escapes the blue-pencilings, the amputations, the transpositions and the imprecations which play their part in whipping into shape the news stories of a day. A degree of confidence is placed in him that is only to be justified on the assumption that he is a better, not a poorer, journalist than the reporters of the city room. It is altogether to his interest that this should be so.

To have the copy that is turned in by the music critic pass through the hands of copy readers who know little or nothing about music is to risk ridiculous changes. Always there is a safeguard in having a second person go over copy for "literals"—the typographical slips and accidental misspellings of names that the writer of the review may be the last one to see, simply because he knows what he intended to write and he reads it that way. Often, an ordinarily careful writer can read and re-read his own copy several times and regard it as letter-perfect. But let him open the paper the next day and merely glance down his column, without actually reading it, and some absurd mistake will fairly leap at him from the printed page. Before he empties the vials of his wrath on the compositors and the proof room, it is always the part of wisdom for him to ask to see the original copy. Otherwise he may have the wind taken out of his sails, when an ink-smudged veteran of the mechanical departments deposits under his nose the telltale script with a red pencil mark encircling for his benefit the oversight of the night before—the one the critic could not possibly have been guilty of—until now!

But this "once-over" for "literals" and kindred slips is not necessarily the business of the copy desk, where pencils are itching to make alterations, if only in punctuation. If the critic has an assistant and the assistant has the time, his perusal of his chief's copy—providing he is not too eager to indicate the ways in which he could have done the job better—is more likely to catch just the errors the critic's eye hurdled over, without otherwise complicating the issue, than that of copy editors who have developed the art and the science of chopping, splicing, re-vamping, toning down or "pepping up" the clutter of stories that is the grist of their mill. Some newspapers have specialists on the copy desk, too. One man may read all stories pertaining to music, because he happens to have musical knowledge. He may be instructed to change nothing in the critic's copy but to look for "outs", misspellings, "literals"—all the little bobbles that plague those who work under high pressure and, perhaps as often, those who do not. With some newspapers, it is assumed that the music critic needs no editing and no verification. This implies the preparation of error-proof copy. It means a persistent checking-up on names, titles, tonalities and opus numbers on the part of the critic; it means punctuation that is fool-proof with regard to alternative constructions in the reading of phrase or clause; frequently it means avoidance on the part of the critic of many things he would like to put on paper but cannot be certain of at the moment of the writing. With an hour in which to prepare his copy, book and score verification may be out of the question.

Still more elementary is the requirement that copy should conform to ordinary newspaper procedure with respect to being clearly typewritten (though occasional exceptions in favor of long-hand still are made in various

newspaper departments, including that of criticism);
the use of soft paper that will cut and paste readily
when the copy-cutter prepares it for the typesetters;
generous margins, top, bottom and sides, permitting of
notations and facilitating pasting; and, appalling as it
may seem to have to mention so obvious a requirement,
the fundamental that all typed copy be *double or triple
spaced and on one side of the paper only*. Murder, may-
hem, arson, incest, miscegenation, cosmic combustion,
almost anything is possible in the office that has to deal
with page on page of single-spaced typing, with the
lines so close together that the insertion of sub-heads is
all but impossible; where paragraphs are a page in
length, and where, as the final straw, both sides of the
paper have been used. In this age, such a thing seems
impossible. But it happens again and again when music
reviews are "farmed out" in cities that do not harbor
journalists capable of dealing adequately with music.
Interlineations, in the form of corrections and after-
thoughts, are troublesome enough. But when the reviewer starts underscoring words calling either for
italics, or entire phrases in capital letters, the need of
some other arrangement begins to be impressed upon his
employer. Sentences that rival paragraphs in length,
interruptive interjections, parenthetical detours, even
misplaced footnotes and barrages of technical terms or
foreign language quotations can have occasional place;
but if they are the rule rather than the exception the
copy either will be reconstructed or a new critic employed.

Aside from questions of vocabulary and style, newspaper writing has certain governing considerations— sensed by every copy-boy who has worked a fortnight in the office of a daily—that often seem elusive to highly intelligent and cultivated persons who know their dailies from reading them, but not how they are made. One is the distinction between *interest* and *importance*. These two about sum up the *raison d'être* for every line that appears in a newspaper. From an April Fool's Day joke to a weighty editorial on international debts, from the fashion comments to the cables on the deliberations of the League of Nations, from the market tabulations to the news of supper clubs, either interest or importance, or both, has assured the survival for publication of that particular item or feature, in competition with a multitude of others that had to be discarded because of too much news.

Most newspaper men have been trained to place interest before importance. The antics of a spectacular character known to everyone in the city may command more space than a famine in Java, for the reason that many more readers are interested. It is not imperative that a book on music criticism should go deeply into this, or dwell on the endless ramifications of an issue variously dealt with by newspapers of widely differing outlook as to what constitutes important or interesting news; but it is of moment to bear in mind that the music review which is lacking in interest is likely to be just so much wasted type. The reviewer may feel that he is dealing with music of importance. But his mirror has failed in its purpose if his readers find that what he has to say about this important music is unreadably dull.

Newspaper writing has various traditions, some fetishes, a plentiful routine, and a few—perhaps too few —tabus. In every sort of reporting, reviewing included, there is the "lead" to consider. Ordinarily the "lead" is not a literary introduction, but a summary of salient facts. Usually, it includes the *who, what, when* and *where* of the news event and perhaps the *how, why* or *how much.* Exceptions are not infrequent, but the ordinary procedure in the preparation of copy is to enlighten the reader at the outset as to what happened, then fill in with details in the subsequent paragraphs. This is not merely a short-cut to the news. It is a device for awakening immediate interest. It is one way of putting *the best foot foremost.* Usually when another way of beginning a story has been substituted for the factual lead, it is because that other way also awakes interest at the start and is, in fact, *a better first foot.*

Only too often there is needless pother about the opening sentence. As every man who has ever worked in a city room knows, a reporter with a simple news story to write will make a dozen starts, often getting no more than twenty words on paper before he has a change of plan in his effort to catch and hold the eye with his "lead". Thus conceived, the "lead" readily degenerates into one of the mannerisms of journalese. But the principle of *the best foot foremost* survives all the absurdities committed in its name; and any one who writes for newspapers, the music critic included, has reason to

ask himself whether he has buried that best foot somewhere down in his review instead of using it to step off
with, blithely and confidently, at the start.

At the risk of appearing to advocate for the music
critic an approach for his writing that the author is well
aware would be extreme even for the police reporter,
let us consider one newspaperman's exaggerated but
none the less illuminative way of impressing the idea of
the best foot upon the cub reporter. No two stories, he
contends, ever are the same. In most instances, it is some
circumstance peculiar to a given story, not a circumstance
to be found in all stories of the same general nature, that
is of first interest. For example, there are many suicides.
The reporter concerned only with getting the facts on
paper would in many instances begin report after report
with the name of the person who had taken his own life.
In one instance, the name might startle the nation. In
another, the name would be utterly meaningless. In the
first instance, obviously the name was the best foot. In
the second, something else surely was of greater interest.
This might be the *time* of the suicide. If so, the story
might begin, "Five minutes after the lapse of his insurance". Or it might be the *place,* "Standing before
the painting of Mona Lisa". It might be the *reason.*
"Because of millinery bills amounting to two thousand
dollars". Or it might be the *method.* "Leaping into a vat
of molten metal". No apologies need be made for the
crudity of these illustrations. They serve their purpose
in supporting the contention that always there is a best
foot and that this best foot many times is the individual

detail that is true only of one story and tends to make that story different, and unique among its fellows. Without attempting to parallel the sort of distinction drawn here, the music critic can at least ask himself the question whether he is beginning his reviews too persistently with a name; and whether, if he were discussing a particular concert with a friend, he would not bring up first, because of first interest, some special consideration that was peculiar to this concert alone.

At any rate he needs to remember the *who, what, when* and *where,* as well as the *how* that is the burden of his opinions. His readers expect the essential facts.

THE WORDING OF JUDGMENTS

In the wording of his judgments, the critic has before him daily opportunities to be a gentleman. The late Henry T. Finck * has passed on to the profession the wise words of an editor who told him never to write about a musician anything he would not be willing to say to that musician's face. Of course no critic goes about telling singers that they don't know how to produce their top tones or reminding violinists that they play persistently sharp. But if he were cornered, and his opinion were necessary to meet the exigencies of the moment, any critic should be able to speak of these and other unwelcome truths without personal offense to the person addressed. Teachers have to do it. Friends and family members can scarcely justify their special relation if they do not, on occasion, inform an artist of faults or tendencies likely to hamper his progress.

The critic, as has been repeated here to the extent of tedium, does not write for the artist but for the readers of his newspaper. This impersonality might seem to justify him in riding rough-shod over whatever he regards

* Henry T. Finck, for forty-three years music critic of the *New York Evening Post*.

as inferior. But that way lies distortion. On paper, the angry word looks and reads unfair, even though it may hit the nail squarely on the head. Passion savors of bias, though it may be passion in a good cause. Leaders of movements and champions of causes are expected to have that sort of bias. Ordinarily, the critic is a spectator and should be free from it. Emotional writing breeds distrust of opinion. The desire to obliterate or to humiliate is difficult to reconcile with impartiality. The crusading critic is likely to become more propagandist than critic. To be feared—that, surely, is not the most enviable status in criticism or the affairs of nations. The desire to sting is attributable to small souls. To be frank and outspoken may mean many things besides rubbing salt in wounds.

The critic's war, ordinarily, is not so much against what is obviously bad or meretricious as against what is mediocre. The critic knows that to encourage the mediocre is to have a hand in filling the garden with weeds so that the flowers cannot grow. He may agree with W. J. Henderson, whose mellow writing may be taken as an object lesson of what criticism should be, that there is too much indulgence and too little severity. But severity does not mean the hurling of epithets. It does not mean bitterness or ridicule. It does not mean barbs that fester. It may mean bluntness, but words can be blunt and still impersonal—even kindly. If the critic were a machine, recording judgments like a barometer or a seismograph, there would be no occasion for any one to feel a whip-lash in anything that was recorded. But since he is not a machine, since he is one human being writing about other human beings for readers who also are human beings, simple humanity is reasonably a part of the critical attitude and of all critical writing.

The whip-cracking critic who builds a reputation for being caustic where others are kind may do music a real service. But he also may do it much harm. After all, it is not the business of the critic to make a reputation for himself as a grand inquisitor, a Torquemado of verbal torment. That way may lie reputation, but if simple justice is sacrificed for the sake of this kind of brilliance, the critic has placed himself in much the same position as the showy virtuoso of the keyboard or the sensational fiddler who contorts everything he plays into a parade of his technical gifts; a show that sometimes is more than a little sadistic in the wrongs inflicted on the music performed.

Irony, only too easily, can be carried over into sarcasm; humor that is too broad or too pointed becomes ridicule; whimsy is converted into caricature. There are some things the critic should say with a smile. The reader cannot see his face. His words must convey the good will behind them. Now and then he will damn, with flat-footed assertions that can never be mistaken for faint praise. But these occasions, too, will afford him the opportunity to damn like a gentleman.

In the wording of judgments, the critic must not attempt to carry water on both shoulders. For him, his opinions are conclusive. Sometimes he can legitimately pass on to others a state of doubt. But when he has a conclusion that satisfies himself, let him eliminate the word "perhaps". It is better to have to change an opinion than to pussyfoot; better to have to retract what is said than never to say anything.

The well-written criticism is worded clearly and can have but one meaning. It meets issues squarely, even if that involves an occasional confession of doubt. It reads easily and does not impose on the ordinarily well-informed reader the obstacle of uncommon technical terms or obscure allusions. It conveys as true a picture of what is criticized as the critic's knowledge and ability will enable him to convey, within the limitations of his space and in the limited writing time at his disposal. If it invites controversy it does so without malice. If it is corrective, its purpose is only to enable those who consult this mirror to see things as they are. If it is informative, it is not with the thought of playing the pedagogue or the pundit. Simplicity, directness, moderation are ordinary badges of good critical writing, with such variations in the direction of a florid or a humorous style as bespeak naturally the personality and particular gifts of the individual. At one extreme stands the brilliant aphorist or word-colorist who sacrifices opinions to style; at the other the drab scholar whose opinions are sound but whose writing is so dull it is hard to read. Between these extremes there is room for innumerable personalities, each giving to his words something that is his own and employing, as justifiably as the novelist, the biographer or the essayist, the attractions of a conscious literary art. If he is not only a writer but a journalist, the critic will find the way to adjust his word pictures to the particular medium for which he writes.

Pitts Sanborn, a critic with a literary flair, in referring to the repetitions likely to intrude upon a critic's reviews if he writes at a single sitting of various events, as, for instance, a concert in the afternoon and an opera at night, has said that there are "the words of the day". They take possession. The writer has to be on his guard against them, lest he repeat them again and again. Tomorrow, his vocabulary grants him a new deal. Today it may hold him in a vise. It is a caution worth bearing in mind. The mirror cannot effectively reflect two or more quite different events in the same terms.

THE ART OF PRAISE—AND FINDING
FAULT

Criticism has been described, rather euphemistically some may feel, as the art of praise. Most musicians of the acquaintance of the writer would regard it as the art of finding fault. The pragmatic truth is that it is the art of both. Being that, it can be rationalized into the status of the first of these generalities, since if there were no fault-finding there could be little art in praise.

In "The Scope of Music", Dr. Percy Buck has this to say of criticism: "The best critic is the person who can find beauty where others have missed it. . . . Where he finds charlatanry he may expose it, and expose it witheringly; but he does not like finding it, and will generally leave it to die alone; and in any case we should hardly call this finding fault".

Writing in the New York Evening Post of which he was then guest critic, Ernest Newman, of London, took occasion to point out in connection with Dr. Buck's thesis that "we can hardly express warm admiration for anything without implicitly finding fault with other things of the same kind"; and adding that "the more the critic knows his job, the more faults he will find, because to his super-delicate senses more things will seem faulty".

Both praise and fault-finding resolve themselves into the exercise of the same faculty, that of discrimination. If occasionally testiness enters in, it is no more to be applauded than ill-temper anywhere else. Mr. Newman reminds us, however, that there are special excuses for testiness on the part of the music critic, when compared to some other mortals; as, for instance, the critic of painting. The music critic is of necessity a lover of music. As such, Mr. Newman postulates, he is "perpetually frustrated in everything he most desires. He has to submit, day after day, to hearing masterpieces murdered or degraded; how would the lover of painting feel, if in his daily walk through a great gallery, this or that favorite picture was in turn found to have been partly painted over by some modern bungler or other!"

So famous a musician as Berlioz, when he turned to the writing of criticism, had much the same complaint to utter. In his Memoirs he is found crying out against the continual perversion of masterpieces and he frets at having to write civilly about the crimes committed in music's name. Debussy, in various critical essays, railed at composers and performers in a manner that certainly was not to be confined within the hyacinth beds of praise. Wagner's critical articles, a source of much needed revenue when he was face to face with the debtors' prison in Paris, were not exactly encomiums; nor was Schumann unreservedly laudatory when Wagner's music, in turn, came up for criticism. If Hanslick was made notorious

by his attacks on Wagner, should he not be acclaimed
for his praise of Brahms?—praise that Wagner was not
willing to bestow—shouting at Nietzsche that the
Brahms score the philosopher had unwarily put before
him was "nothing but scraps of Handel, Schumann and
Mendelssohn, bound in calf!"

The test of criticism is not that it praise much or little, or dwell lightly or heavily upon faults, but that it be
sound as to both praise and fault-finding, in their relation one to the other, so that the critical mirror's reflection turn out an honest one, rather than some distorted
image with an excess of praise or a one-sided cataloguing
of faults. As to what is constructive and what is destructive, it may be wise to bear in mind what W. J. Henderson has written in speaking particularly of the attitude
of the press toward the débutante. The following is
quoted from a Saturday discourse in the New York
Sun:

After many years of experience in musical criticism, the writer
is convinced that nothing is so reprehensible as the encourage-
ment of young people without talent. . . . If newspaper criticism went after debutantes with an ax there might be something
to say about its evil effects; but it does not do that. It goes after
them with bouquets and works incalculable harm—far more
than it could with a bludgeon. Brutal criticism reacts upon itself;
facile flattery persuades mediocrity that it will do well to spend
more dollars in hiring halls and managers. . . . Severe criticism is reserved for the great personages of the musical world.
No debutant is ever belabored as Mr. Toscanini, or Mr. Pader-
ewski or Miss Ponselle is. When the great do not sustain the
level of their greatness either grief or rage or both spring up

in the critical breast and the English language gets some considerable exercise.

This is the practice. Theoretically, the critic has but one standard, one for the great and small alike. Theory and practice are seldom completely one in the affairs of humans. Only the machine is completely devoid of chivalry. We repeat, the critic is not a machine.

VOCABULARY AND STYLE

The timpanist must love the drum, the writer must love the word. The writer may scorn the ornate and the precious in literary phrase-building. If he does, it will be because he has a passion for words that are simple, forthright and rugged. They are his drums and he plays upon them. Poet or pragmatist, impressionist or realist, visionary or fact-finder, the writer has no other medium for his thoughts. Often enough, the words are thoughts. In going out to meet the music which he is called upon to hear, the critic may be thinking the words he later will write. Sometimes he may almost be said to *hear* the words, so close is their relation to the sounds that are being analyzed behind the ear. To have no feeling for words, to regard them merely as workaday tools, with no life or significance of their own, merely as symbols like numerals or the letters of the alphabet, or as so many algebraic or geometrical characters to enable a problem-worker to arrive at a conclusion, is a calamity for any journalist, the music critic by no means excepted. Not only is his writing doomed to be difficult, dull and wooden, but he is cheated of the pleasure of his toil. If he writes well, with a touch of imagination and stir, he, too, may consider himself something of an artist. Take from him the pigments of his words and he is at best a draughtsman. His mirror reflects only lines. Without verbal color, the thoughts he passes on to his readers are almost certain to be seen pedantic, pale and unfruitful.

By the critic's words you come to know the man. They tell you more of him than the features of his face. It is by them that you perceive the workings of his brain, the character of his emotional reactions, the degree of earnestness and sincerity in his approach. To go further and attempt to measure his cultural breadth by the extent and nature of his vocabulary would be dangerous. But the taste with which he expresses himself, whether in the simplest terms or the most erudite, is a fair measure of the taste with which he listens to music. Virtuosity is by no means synonymous with taste. Every breach of taste possible to the virtuoso fiddler is possible to the virtuoso writer. But just as no one will begrudge the sensational violinist the exceptional technique that he so flagrantly misuses, so no admirer of clear and beautiful writing should resent or deplore an amazing stock of words, however much a flashy parade of unusual adjectives may cheapen the character of a review.

At any rate, the man with too many words is the rare exception. Most writers have need of fine distinctions that their store of similes does not quite supply. In the effort to avoid the cliché, to escape eternal repetition of themselves and of others, reviewers of musical events struggle endlessly to find words and phrases that are fresh and animated, only to be thrown back on some well-worn expression that seems the only thing there is to say. Only rarely will be found such writers as Philip Hale, Lawrence Gilman and W. J. Henderson, for whom words seem to fall in line and march to their appointed destination as if they had been created for that particular service and nothing else would do. Mr. Hale's words seem the inevitable ones. The rare quality of Mr. Gilman's analytical prose brings it to the borders of poetry. Sometimes, in writing about music, he is more the musician, one feels, than was the composer. For some of us there is no such beauty in Stravinsky's tone-poem, "Le Rossignol", as in its annotator's word-music of the nightingale singing in deserted gardens. W. J. Henderson is at once the admiration and despair of his colleagues. He has rid writing of its last suggestions of effort, by perfecting a technique that reads as if it took care of itself. He goes straight to some issue, paragraph by paragraph, sentence by sentence, and, in the concentrated clarity of his style, word by word. There is no waste, no padding, no clutter of circuitous phrases. He says precisely what he wishes to say, no more, no less. Yet he is never curt, never spare. The amplitude of his ideas prevents that. His is a style as mellow and easy as it is precise and clear. The sentence structure, with each sentence a complete idea in itself, yet clearly related to what precedes and follows, explains much of this. But at the bottom of all is the word. Of all critics who have written for American readers, not excepting the brilliant James Gibbons Huneker and the razor-edged Ernest

Newman, none has had a happier faculty for finding the exact and illuminative term. The scholarly Richard Aldrich * also had a way of characterizing by a word a quality or an attribute of performance that would seem to require a phrase.

That the love of words can lead a reviewer, particularly a young one, into excesses bordering on the grotesque is not to be disputed. But that can be remedied. A lack of a feeling for the color and the infinite variety of words is much more serious. At one time, the youth of the land were obsessed by the purple patches of Huneker, whose essays on musical subjects were scarcely to be read without a lexicon at the elbow. Of this prodigiously gifted writer it was said, satirically, that each night before going to bed he devoured a page of an unabridged Webster. Unusual words were to be found in his more extended discussions in such profusion as to suggest that they had been sprinkled there from a pepper shaker. His writings were pageants, "armies with banners" not unlike the battle in the Strauss "Heldenleben", as that orchestral orgy appeared to him. Words were articles of faith, ikons of worship, glimpses behind the veil, flaming prophecies, disembodied spirits, elemental forces, infinities, the destiny of man! He wrote processionals of them. And for a time he was read in the hinterland as possibly no other New York critic ever had been read.

That all aspiring young critics wanted to be Hunekers was not surprising. It was not to be expected that they

---

* Richard Aldrich, music critic of *The New York Times*, 1908–1924.

should see at once that this was a style so personal it could not be duplicated successfully in the same field. An Edgar Saltus could exist alongside a Huneker because he dealt with quite other material. But one Huneker at a time was quite enough for readers of music criticism. We may doubt that this word-worship was in any lasting degree harmful. Some young fellows got themselves laughed at in editorial sanctums and went away, perhaps with hurt feelings. But nothing that they were moved to do to enlarge their vocabularies—even when the word they tried to apply to a quality of voice was a medical or metallurgical one—took anything from them. They gained something—the word and the lesson of using words where they belong.

Obviously, the limited vocabulary limits utterance, the extended vocabulary facilitates it. To increase one's store of words is a laudable ambition on the part of any writer, young or old. Those who have retentive memories and do much reading are continually adding to their reserve supply, without realizing, perhaps, that the mind has worked like a pair of tweezers in extracting a particular term from its context and depositing it in its proper mental receptacle. It may not be used for years, but there it is. The wider the reading the more generously the memory is stored with these incidental acquisitions. Fortunate the writer who has this faculty of picking up words without labor. He is likely to use them in the same way. The man too conscious of his treasures may force them to do duty where they are not wanted. Particularly in brief reviews of routine events, the unusual word may obtrude annoyingly. The character and length of the discussion, the nature of the publication in which it is printed, the cultural level of the bulk of readers, all have their bearing on a choice of words. The newspaper review should leave the family dictionary free for use by those who solve the daily crossword puzzle.

The critic, however, and especially the critic in the making, need not be ashamed if, in lieu of the gradual accumulation of words by wide reading, he devotes a part of his labors to the dictionary, the thesaurus, or any compilation and collation that serves as a short cut to the acquirement of words. Where and how Shakespeare accumulated his unmatched vocabulary is one of the many mysteries of the man; it would remain no less one of the marvels of the plays and sonnets if he had culled his word stock laboriously from a book.

It is not the purpose of the author to recommend or decry any writing "style". The critic's writing will reflect the artist and the man. The essentials are that it be clear and that it possess reader interest. Beyond that, let the reviewer fulfil his obligations to himself, his employers and the art. This he must do with words, phrases, clauses, sentences and paragraphs, as well as with opinions and the knowledge he possesses of the musical art. He will write well if he can. And he will write his own way.

BOOK FIVE

THE LIFE

THE CRITIC'S FRIENDS

The distinguished English practitioner, Ernest New-man, has commented on the music critic's inability, al-most unique among the professions, to make many real friendships among the people with whom his life has to be spent. We are free to infer that stevedores and long-shoremen, not composers and conductors; seven-day bicycle racers and truck gardeners, not singers and pian-ists, are the critic's rightful companions. To know mu-sicians intimately is precarious; to permit ties of affec-tion to bind critic and musician together is to place in jeopardy all that the critic stands for as a disinterested spectator, an impartial adjudicator, a truthful, unflat-tering, yet intensifying mirror. The critic may come to feel that it is best for him to avoid artists; to meet them accidentally, if it must be, but preferably not at all; to limit contacts with those whom chance has brought into his life; to decline all social favors from them; to regard them always impersonally, mindful of the journalistic axiom so sharply put by the political writer of a New York newspaper, who, when upbraided by an office-seeker because of the hostile attitude of his paper to-ward this man, replied: "Sir, to me, you represent only so much copy". It is sometimes the workaday answer that turneth away wrath!

"So much copy"—an image to be reflected—a work in sound to be transliterated into words—notes, musical forms, harmonies, orchestration, fingers, pedals, scale passages, breath control, double stops, balances, inflections, temperament, taste, style—the man or the woman of it—the genius or the plodding artisan—a prince or a pauper of the art—but in the end, "just so much copy" —a judgment to be formed, a description or an analysis to be written—a mirror to reflect the essentials and pass them on.

If critics were either super-men or machines, if they were other than ordinary human clay, close friendships with musicians might be as harmless—even as beneficial in the practice of their profession as they could be stimulating in spheres remote from music. Unfortunately and fortunately, critics are not machines, even though here and there may be found one not so certain that he is not a superman. There are egotists in other professions, too, not to exclude the vocation of the musical artist. There have been, and are, humble critics, even painfully reverent of the art, and tediously conscious of their limitations in the effort to deal adequately with that art. Egotism and humility are badges of erring man. Neither is a property of the machine.

To seek to favor a friend is the natural impulse of every normally constituted man or woman. To avoid favoring a friend is the conscientious desire of the critic who takes his obligations seriously. It is expected of him, and rightfully, that he will give to a complete stranger precisely the same treatment that he will accord the crony of many years. But, human being that he is, can he always count on the impartiality of his reactions? Can he altogether subdue the desire to make excuses for his friend's deficiencies? Can he be certain that he is not seizing with an undue eagerness on meritorious details that would be noted but would not appear nearly so conclusive or important, in the composition or the performance of one in whom he had no personal interest? Critics, able, honest, just, have been known to evade flat judgments on the work of those they have known too well— they have deferred opinions for future hearings—then flashed out with sharp, immediate appraisal on the work of a stranger quite as difficult to place and analyze at a single sitting. Probably the avoidance of the issue in the first instance was more unconscious than conscious. At its worst, it had its justifiable side. It was human. But it was poor journalism. It disappointed and in a sense cheated the reader. What had become of the dictum, "Just so much copy"?

By no means is it to be taken for granted, however, that the critic will favor the musical performer or composer he happens to know. His desire *not* to favor him may cause the critic to "lean over backwards" in the effort to be fair. Innumerable, no doubt, are the instances in which faults are more particularized, virtues given less positive emphasis, than would have been the case if the critic had been dealing with a stranger. Sometimes the very tone of the review betrays an anxiety not to be friendly, not to go too far in a performer's behalf, not to exhibit a personal interest that the critic realizes he should not feel. So, again, he cheats his readers—and because of a false position created by the need of sitting as censor on himself. Occasionally, a critic declines to review a concert for personal reasons—sending an assistant in his stead. Once more it is the reader—the critic's real excuse for being—who stands to lose. If this was a concert the first critic should have covered, the personal reasons which stood in the way ought never to have been.

But how could they have been obviated? In some instances, it would seem, only by making a hermit of the critic—certainly a heavy price to pay for impartiality and scarcely the life for the man of the world the sound critic almost inevitably must be. A compromise is inevitable. Critics *do* know musicians—but warily. If they are wise, they avoid what contacts they can; they accept, with a multitude of reservations and safeguards, what they cannot avoid. They may seek, and do seek, friendships in the directions of their special musical interests, their particular hobbies, their individual affections—as happens when critics turn propagandists for what they consider neglected genius. But this involves the extension of the critical function already discussed, with its attendant danger. Only too often it is the Hanslick *against* Wagner, who is the advocate *for* Brahms; or the Finck who can have no admiration *for* Brahms, who can say no word *against* Grieg. The pro-Mahlerite is apt to be little interested in Sibelius. The Sibelius ad-

vocate may find himself *resisting* what he regards as
propaganda for Bruckner. All such special interests
may result in enlightenment and progress—even in the
justice that must be dear to every well-tempered critic's
heart—but they have only to acquire a degree too much
of momentum to run away with judgment and unsettle
the balance that is the anchor of impartiality and, let us
put it, *unconscious* honesty.

But, sighs the critic, I could learn so much if I could
talk over all these questions, all these details, seeking
out the hidden reasons, the undisclosed aims and aspira-
tions, the secrets of effects and the means used to ends,
with the men I really respect—the musicians, executive
or creative, who by virtue of their peculiar relation to
the music at issue, and their vastly more specialized
training, could take me behind the curtain, so to speak.
Again we are in the sphere of *indirect data,* vastly educative but sometimes profoundly misleading. There is
the danger of a hardening of the musical arteries in this
sort of communion, especially if it leads to a personal
attachment and a conviction that because the one for
whom this attachment exists is a notable musician he
must be right.

Let us consider for a moment what it means to be
close friends with a conductor, one of undoubted eminence. How easily it can be argued that surely he, with
his exceptional musicianship, his vast experience, his
intensive study of scores, can be looked to as an authority on questions of tempi in the performance of symphonies. For the conductor, his convictions with regard

to these tempi are more or less final. He feels them thus, he cannot feel them another way. Other conductors who play this music faster or slower are entitled to their lights, of course, but the fact remains that their tempi are too fast or too slow! They must be true to their own feelings, but they are wrong! With the conductor, he who hesitates is lost. There can be no equivocations in interpretation. Before his players, before his audiences, before his critics, the conductor's attitude must admit of no doubt; first of all he must utterly convince himself that he doesn't "mean maybe"; and beyond and above all, he must believe in himself and in the inevitable correctness of that expression of himself which goes into the determination of his tempi.

But the critic, mayhap, could have had a considerable choice of conductors when it came to choosing a friend who also would be his rock of refuge in this question of tempi. If he had chosen another, that other might have been of equal eminence, equally experienced, equally intensive in his study of his scores; above all, equally convinced of the unalterable finality and justness of his conceptions. Yet the tempi of number two would be all wrong to number one; and number one always either fast or slow to number two. It is one thing for a student to grasp eagerly at these straws as he sits at the feet of a master in learning the art of conducting, hopeful that one day he may carry on the traditions of a Nikisch, a Safonoff, a Walter or a Reiner in his own concerts. It would be quite another thing for a critic to condemn Mr. Toscanini, Mr. Furtwängler, Mr. Stokowski or Mr.

Koussevitsky because their tempi were not the tempi of any of these other conductors.

We have discussed a composite standard, particularly in criticizing opera. Its application to orchestral performances is not difficult to reason out. The critic's sense of the justness of tempi is more often the result of hearing many performances, with many modifications of pace, than of an ironclad conception at the outset, corresponding to a conductor's determination of what the tempi must be. For the critic, it is altogether desirable that there be something of fluidity in these conceptions. In an accumulation of experience, the earliest conceptions may change; somewhere along the way—perhaps in the first year of his practice of the profession, perhaps the tenth or the twentieth—a conductor may bring a revelation that will cause the critic to wonder why what he has heard was not disclosed before. The critic may feel that then, for the first time, his conviction as to tempi has become fixed and final. But do the other conductors change their convictions? Where would the critic have stood in judging the man who brought him his revelation if the critic, like these other conductors, had been set and final in his opinion from the first?

The critic cannot afford to ignore the Lincoln aphorism that men can differ and both be right. To draw too liberally on the specialized knowledge of particular musicians, whatever their great gifts, as a critic may do only too readily if he numbers these musicians among his intimates, is to risk being as one-sided in his estimates as his musical friends probably would be if they were

called upon to sit in critical judgment of the performances of their rivals. (Possibly, at that, conductor
criticizing conductor would illustrate only too dis-
appointingly how readers are denied their due when the
self-conscious critic goes in for leaning over backwards
in dealing with a friend.)

There are other irritations and tribulations almost
certain to arise from free and easy association with
artists, each artist intent on advancing an individual
career. Favors are asked that have to be refused. They
seem just to the artist—the critic really should want to
favor the deserving—and bad feeling may result. There
are the inevitable discussions in which the critic, being
human, would prefer not to say to an artist's face what
is so much more impersonally said in print. Questions
are asked that the critic would prefer not to answer. He
must either dissemble or assume a brutal frankness that
is distasteful.

To pay compliments, socially, that do not square with
what a critic has to write, professionally, is of itself re-
pugnant enough to cause a sensitive critic to avoid gatherings where compliments seem to be the life of the
party. Now and then, perhaps frequently, critics do
attend such gatherings. Sometimes it is from choice.
There may be no embarrassments; only a little banter
where the ice is thinnest and some really felicitous chat
about a multitude of common interests, including music
and the performance of music. But behind the screen,
even then, may be a trace of anxiety, of apprehension,
of wondering "what next". The man of the world meets

such issues as they arise. He may have the wit, the poise, the art, the charm to convert every threatened contretemps into a triumph of good fellowship. He may relish doing so. But to be forever fencing is to be drawing pretty heavily on the vital energies the critic has urgent need of in his writing, his listening, his thinking and his limitless reading and research. Against the possible access of knowledge resulting from close associations with musicians, he must weigh an accumulation of petty incidents, petty discomfitures, petty worries. It is for each member of the critical profession to make his choice. If he agrees with Mr. Newman on the way the cards of friendship are stacked against him, where musicians are concerned, he need not fall back completely on the stevedores and longshoremen, the seven-day bicycle racers and the truck gardeners. There are still poets, painters, sculptors, novelists, playwrights, educators and brilliant fellow-journalists to offer him a generous choice of intimates quite as likely to supplement his knowledge, and add to his background; thus playing a part in his cultural and professional growth no less consequential than the good things to be derived from close association with musicians.

The author realizes that this chapter may easily be construed as quixotic. He has not sought to expound a rule. Each man's life is his own. Professional and social contacts do not mean precisely the same for any two individuals. One man needs a protective armor another can go without. There have been critics, noted ones, who were the hub of the musical wheel. Their soirées have drawn about them the distinguished, the popular, the beautiful. To debate further whether they were the better or the worse critics for their associations would be a vain proceeding, since no two instances would be really parallel. But as this entire study of music criticism is, in effect, a succession of warnings about the pitfalls that beset the path, the note of caution here sounded is consistent with an outline that must remain suggestive and discussional, rather than a prescribed or even recommended course of action. If love laughs at locksmiths, friendship vaults over hedges.

THE CRITIC AND AMERICAN MUSIC

With the issue of American music confronting him, the American critic must make one clear and decisive choice. Either he will become in some manner or degree a propagandist and friend at bar, or he will decline to draw any distinctions whatever between the music of the country in which he lives and works and has his pride of citizenship, and that of any other country under the sun. Any sort of vacillation between the two positions, now the one, now the other, is likely to be fatal to respect. The campaigner usually commands respect, even if he is not altogether fair. Indeed, what leader worthy of his salt in any controversy, whether one of music or politics, is likely to be conspicuous for fairness?

Ordinarily, the critic's business is to be fair. But the same equipment which qualifies a trained and experienced listener to formulate sound and impartial judgments may enable him to play exceedingly well the role of intercessor, prophet or exegete. These doubtless are extra-critical functions, as the fundamentals of the profession have been viewed here. More may be accomplished by some such departure, in particular instances, than by rigid adherence to the principles of neutrality, as between the music of one land and that of another. The question of which attitude will result in the most good is, however, a human question, not a critical one. It is for the man to decide, not the critic. The moment he turns propagandist, the man ceases to be a critic. He may have a dual function, a dual personality even, in reconciling his critical duties with his extra-critical propaganda. It has been done. Doubtless in varying degrees and in varying ways, it will continue to be done. But the objections and the risks will remain. So will the question whether the greatest service that can be done American music is not the service of a detached, completely disinterested, altogether non-national criticism, concerned only with music and not with the place in which the composers of that music dwell or were born.

Undoubtedly certain foreign countries have fostered their own music with a more zealous self-interest than America has done. Undoubtedly what has been achieved to give the home composer a place in the sun has in some degree been attributable to a sympathetic attitude of the press. In Norway and Czecho-Slovakia, to name but two of a number of European countries that have attracted attention for the character and quantity of their musical output, there assumably has been a less exacting attitude on the part of critics than has obtained in the chief American cities, though the composers and the critics of those countries might argue quite the contrary. That less notable music has been given to the world under these circumstances, as compared to that which has flowered in Germany in the face of severe and often hostile criticism may have no very direct application to the issue. There is only the circumstance to consider that no amount of fostering ever made a Wagner, a Brahms or a Schubert. Nor did the lack of it, so far as the tragedies of music have been disclosed, ever keep a composer of their order from attaining his place.

Probably most American composers would insist that all they demand of a critic is that he be fair and not take it for granted that because a work lacks the European hallmark it must be inferior. They ask respect, they ask knowledge of their aims, they ask to be understood. It is in meeting the demand to be understood that the critic may be called on to take a rather one-sided position as regards American music, in competition with other music. "Understanding" may imply standing shoulder to shoulder with the composer and making his ends the critic's own, in a way the critic would not feel justified in doing when listening to foreign music perhaps no better, perhaps no worse. The musical intercessor is apt to find himself in this position. He makes the composer's ends his own. He ceases to reflect, he projects. The *indirect data* of what he knows about purposes, aesthetics and ideals may overshadow in importance the *direct data,* as supplied by the music. He may find himself dealing with this music according to very different criteria than those that govern him when the imported music of the Norwegian or the Czech composer has to make its effect by sound alone, with no such back-stage information helping the composer to be "understood".

The common complaint, of course, is that the foreign

work receives the better treatment, and because it is foreign. Whether this has been true of the past, or, if true then, is true now, could be disputed endlessly with nothing that could be regarded as a preponderance of proof attainable by either side. Today, however, it is feasible to seek for reasons why foreign music should be regarded as any better than our own, without prejudice to the position of composer, critic or lay listener.

Undoubtedly there was a time, and not many years removed, when so few American composers were craftsmen of the skill of the leading composers of Europe as to supply some real basis for a prejudice against American works as yet unperformed. The conductors who conscientiously examined many manuscripts and rejected most of them can testify to that. There was an obvious difference between the general level of European writing for orchestra and American. That is no longer true, or, if true, is true in less degree. Few new American works of recent years have been taken to task primarily for a lack of technical grasp. For that matter, few European. Work after work, domestic as well as foreign, has exhibited qualities of workmanship that called for critical commendation at the same time that other attributes of equal or greater importance were declared lacking—such as freshness, power or significance of thematic material, or the fitness of this material for the uses to which it was put. Since American composers learned how to score, there has been little to choose in orchestration, between the average American novelty and the average European. A Strauss, a Ravel,

a Respighi, or a Schoenberg is so individual that he has
to be left out of this reckoning. But the instrumentation
of the contemporary English, German, French, and
Italian writers who occupy places at all comparable to
the place of the better known Americans does not cause
the work of the latter to be singled out as the butt of
invidious comparisons. Possibly, agreement would be
reached that the scoring of the Europeans, generally
speaking, has more of polish and finesse; but it may be
questioned whether this feeling obtrudes itself upon the
consciousness of the critic more than on the lay listener
who may never think of scoring for its own sake. The
differences between man and man and work and work
are too numerous and pronounced to permit of any very
sound generalization, either way.

Granting that the American composer has come of
age, therefore, in his use of materials, not only as to orchestration but the handling of structure, the reviewer is
brought face to face with two questions that may be more
definitely inter-related than at first seems true of them.
It is these that cast the doubt, if there exists a doubt,
on the work that has not yet been heard; the doubt
that many advocates of American music believe acts as
a barrier of prejudice against the impartial hearing
ordinarily given European works. The first of these is
the question whether the American composer, good
craftsman or no, has it in him to create thematic material of distinction. The second is, can he have a style of
his own, or is it not more likely that he will present a
succession of imitations of the styles of other men.

Reminiscence and eclecticism are common enough charges everywhere. But they have been so common as to be almost universal regarding American music.

The inter-relation of these two doubts pertains certainly to America's basic lack of musical material older than its musical art—the material that determines the thing called nationalism in music. The need of it has driven composers to the not very tractable tribal lays of the red men and to the too-facile work songs and spirituals of the negroes. A critical question remains whether this material, alike in both instances, is not as external and adoptive on the part of the white American of to-day, in his attempts to make use of it, as would be the Bavarian folk-tune or the Russian barge-song that would subject him immediately to the trite accusation of writing other men's music rather than his own. Is Indian or negro music something that is *a part of him,* in the sense that music sprung of the soil is a part of the Italian, the German, the Russian, the Norwegian or the Czech?

The importance of this question to the critic is not so much one of the possibility of achieving a national style or idiom—since he may very well be convinced that nationalism is not nearly so important as good music—as of the seed that is implanted within, the blossoming that is in the blood, the heritage that is something to be given out rather than acquired by the peoples who had the tunes first, the art afterward. He may feel that the inability to create significant and beautiful themes is governed by the same considerations that cause the American composer to write like an Italian, a Russian, a German, a Frenchman or a Pole, and more probably, like several of these. The national root is the theme root, the style chiefly the growth and flowering of art upon that root. The composer without a folk music below the strata of his own being—as distinguished from that which he may pick up outside of it—may be no melodist for the reason that he has no melodic root. He must build on the roots of other men, or not at all. If he be one rooted in another soil, as Victor Herbert was, he may make use of what he brings with him when he uproots and transfers his entire musical tree. Such instances might be multiplied indefinitely. An outstanding one is that of Ernest Bloch.

It is not the purpose here, however, to advance this or any other consideration as argument in denial of the highest possibilities for American music. To lean too heavily on such theories is almost to place the critic in the role of a hostile propagandist, even if he keep his propaganda to himself. He can only have an open mind if he can contrive to hear each composition separately, as a work illustrative of no theory of his own, but of the structural grasp, the harmonic individuality, the technical resource and the melodic inspiration of a man no more hampered by his nationality than would be a native of Munich, Bucharest, Stockholm, or Bordeaux. He may do well to listen much more assiduously for evidence of thematic or harmonic independence than for conformity or nonconformity to any supposed national style. Eclecticism, imitation, reminiscence, multiplicity of styles can be justly criticised in any work, American or foreign. To point out that they are present is merely to fulfil the mirror function. There may be a "higher criticism" in substituting something less disinterested and impartial for the mirror; something like the torch or the cudgel, the revelation of the prophetic word, but it is to be suspected that this "higher criticism", valuable as it may be, is something else and not criticism at all.

If we turn to the past and consider the men of genius who may seem to have needed intercessors and champions to fight for them the battle against stupidity and malice, we find that really all that was needed, as far as criticism was concerned, was the competent mirror—the mirror that reflected the musical *truth*. Perhaps that truth is one thing to one generation, another to the next. But stupidity and malice never were part of the truth in any era. Nor did inability to hear melody, where there was ample melody to be heard, or to discover form, where form was readily to be found, or to sense the poetry and humanity of works primarily poetic and human, mean anything other than the inability to find and reflect the truth; the inability of the critic to fulfill his mirror function—when that was all he need have done to give any neglected or misprized master his due. Let the critic view the American music of the past in this light. He should then have a clear outlook as to the part he is to play in the American music of the present and the future.

THE TOILSOME ROAD

Somewhere, at some time, a critic of music may have been so supremely the egotist as to go on to the end convinced that he knew it all and that his word was law. How enviable his lot! How many the pangs of conscience and the fevers of doubt he was spared! To be Jove and to loose one's thunderbolts in godlike assurance that they will strike only where there is deadwood to be splintered and cleared away, what a life! Though this critic may have been, we do not know his name. Plenty have sought to pontificate, often to the advancement of the art; quite as often to their own stultification in the eyes of those who came after. But we wonder how many of these were men who wrote brave words rather than equivocate, expressing honestly the judgments that were the best they could form, the while they were secretly troubled at heart over what they felt neither they nor any other man could regard as an altogether adequate preparation for the task.

Critics, it may be assumed, have substantially the same confidence in themselves as other men and women pursuing the vocations of their choice. They could not long command the respect of their readers or their em-

ployers, much less the composers and artists they write
about, if they hesitated and apologized over their ver-
dicts at every turn. They can have no apologies to make
for performing the mirror function as best they can.
But once they have passed the cocksure stage of their
half-baked youth, they are likely to have their faith in
their own qualifications for their mission tested so severely as to make their braver words seem brave indeed.

The critic of normal sensibilities and average pride
of self—conceding that he does exist and is probably in
a majority among his fellows—will have many a moment
of disgust and even despair; disgust with himself, despair as to his competence for his task. Could he really
exhaust one little aspect of the art with which he has to
deal, he would have achieved the super-human. But he
must spread his capacities over a veritable infinity of
related, but more and more specialized, manifestations
—from the acoustics of an auditorium to the costume
of a ballet dancer; from the diction of a singer to the
aesthetic of an age of machines; from the scoring of a
Rimsky-Korsakoff to the mystery of the immortal beloved of a Beethoven; from the riddle of a prima donna
to that of Elgar's "Enigma" Variations. And find always, even regarding the prima donna, that he stands
only on the frontiers of what he ought to know!

In moments of confidence, a little morbid or maudlin
perhaps, or a little hopeful of reassurance and consolation, one reviewer may bewail to another his utter dissatisfaction with himself. He may berate himself as a
charlatan and really half mean it. He may view his

opinions as petty intrusions, his writings as mere word-spinning and pretty thin word-spinning at that. He may suffer, or imagine that he suffers, the torments of the damned because he has just written something he no longer believes to be so. A colleague's greater insight or additional research has stung him to the quick. A musician who knew a particular score as he now feels he should have known it, but did not, has caused him to feel a certain emptiness in the pit of the stomach by reason of a chance remark about cuts or restorations of cuts that had never entered his head as he listened intent on other aspects of a performance. He is desolated by the discovery that others have seen what he could not see in a first disclosure of new music; though repetitions of the work later may convince him that what they saw never was really there. He is forever girding up his loins against himself. He must combat any weakness of doubts and misgivings. At times he is on the verge—or thinks he is—of throwing up his job.

Then, some well-meaning soul puts the everlasting question: "Don't you get tired of music, listening to it every night?" He bristles and stiffens. Doesn't a book-keeper get tired of adding figures every day? Doesn't a doctor get tired of setting broken limbs? Doesn't a sales-man get tired of talking insurance or soliciting advertising? Would he be any less tired doing any of those things? He murmurs his devout thanks for the life he is permitted to lead and goes back to his task of listening, thinking and striving for brave words.

His justification he finds in the many who know so

much less than he. At every turn he is conscious of specialists, who, in their particular line, could tell him more
than he has learned, though he is by no means sure that
they could apply that same knowledge as well as he.
This much vanity, surely, may be permitted to him. But
for every such specialist off on a sidepath where none
but other specialists may be expected to follow, a multitude of relatively simple folk, variously informed or
uninformed, will be found trudging along the main road.
The conscience-stricken reviewer discovers he must look
back to these. He is well ahead of the great majority of
those for whom he writes. After all, then, he has something to tell them, something useful, helpful, illuminat-
ing, to impart.

At the very moment he is castigating himself for not
being immeasurably further along, and for having failed
to explore to the limit those side paths on which the specialists are hunting wild boar or chasing butterflies, he
discovers envying, even trustful and hopeful eyes fixed
upon him from among the hordes of wayfarers who
would consider themselves altogether fortunate to have
traversed the road so far as he. The many may envy him
the fragmentary knowledge he considers so inadequate,
in thinking, conscience-stricken, of the few.

Letters of praise or letters of abuse—the latter even
more than the former—convince him that he has a place
in the scheme of things. The conservative layman who
berates his *bête-noir* of "modern" music because it has
"no form"—on the basis of a performance the night
before of some discordant and most unsympathetic com-

position which happened to be an example of the modern tendency toward compact and hard-edged structure, more severe in its form than the romantic efflorescences of the conservative's own true day—increases the critic's respect for his mirror. There is something to pass on to that man. And his name is legion.

It is a toilsome road. The by-paths cannot be altogether ignored. Some may present such enticing vistas that the critic, intentionally or no, himself becomes a specialist, a slayer of wild boars or a chaser of butterflies. But he cannot explore them all with anything like equal interest and thoroughness. He must get back to the main highway, with its dust and puddles and the obstructions that those who went on ahead only partly removed. He must expect to be passed by some who can move faster than he. They may shout back to him of the shining vistas that lie ahead. When he reaches them, they have in some way paled. How will it be for those who are toiling on a league or two in the rear?

The longer he tramps the longer he realizes there is no end, not even any goal; except that of the day when he shall lay down his pen. There is more beyond than can ever be put behind. The horizon has widened, but it retreats with every step. The pilgrim may come to regard himself in the light of the explorer who establishes food caches for those who will follow him, expecting them to go farther than he. If he serves only as signpost, pointing the way, he may feel that not in vain has he stuffed his life with books, sounds and words. He may even regard himself as something of a martyr—and, martyr-like, find that he has had a corking good time in sacrificing what he wasn't much interested in anyway, for the sake of what in his heart of hearts he knew was the great passion of his life.

To listen—to write—to find his kind of self-expression, even as the creative or executive artist finds his—was it such a bad life, after all?